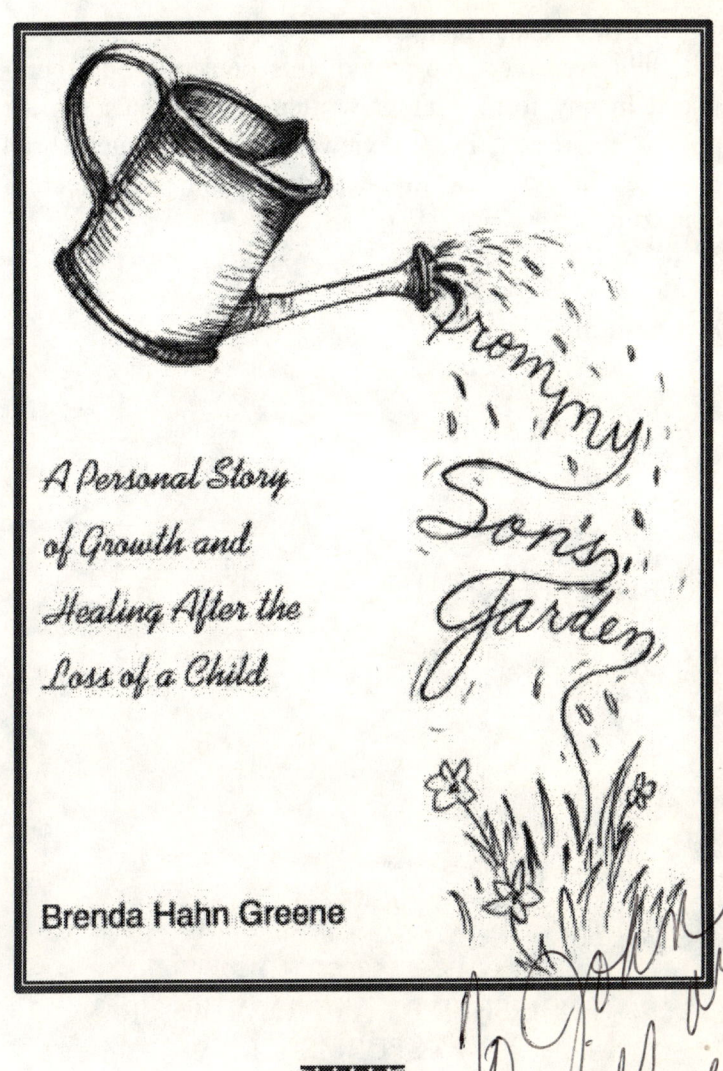

From my Son's Garden

A Personal Story of Growth and Healing After the Loss of a Child

Brenda Hahn Greene

AmErica House
Baltimore

© 2001 by Brenda Hahn Greene.
All rights reserved. No part of this book may be reproduced in any form without written permission from the publishers, except by a reviewer who may quote brief passages in a review to be printed in a newspaper or magazine.

First printing

Illustrated by Cheryl H. Hahn

ISBN: 1-58851-410-2
PUBLISHED BY AMERICA HOUSE
BOOK PUBLISHERS
www.publishamerica.com
Baltimore

Printed in the United States of America

TABLE OF CONTENTS

Foreward 7
Acknowledgments 9
Introduction 11
Getting Started 17
Remembering the Day of My Son's Death 23
The First Year After His Death 33
The Second Year After His Death 67
The Third Year After His Death 95
Healing Thoughts to Remember 119

John Robert (Joby) Greene
March 18, 1981—May 18, 1997

Foreword
by
Sally Downham Miller, Ph.D.

(Author of *Mourning and Dancing*, and *Mourning and Dancing for Schools: A Grief and Recovery Sourcebook for Students, Teachers and Parents*)

Writing is an amazing gift, because once penned the words go on giving. *From My Son's Garden* is a gift of passionate writing that blesses not only its readers, but also the writer and the memory of the one about whom the story was written. Writing about loss and grief is like a calliope releasing its steam through whistles that makes beautiful sounds; it is a cathartic release that gives voice to that which can no longer be touched. This mother's love and the ways in which she honors her son Joby's life are gripping and exhilarating. It is an honest account of her hard work processing her grief and helping her son's friends as they find their way on a similar journey.

This is a story that will touch both parents and friends who have been similarly stricken. It will help them to feel less alone. It will inform and direct others who stand by and wonder what to say and do. It will make you cry and laugh and marvel at all of the good that has come from memorializing and remembering the life of one who left too soon. It will testify to the healing that has come to one who is willing to do the hard, brave work in finding a healthy path through living with loss. It conveys the great gift of a parent's love, which knows that there are some losses we live with for a lifetime, without living a diminished life. There are some gifts you just can't wait to give and this story is one.

Acknowledgments

I never thought I would reach this point in my personal journey of grief. I never could have accomplished this without my husband, my children, and our extended family members. I hope my sisters and my brother know how much I have counted on them for support and love that they have unconditionally given me. Uncle John (Joby's godfather) and Aunt Suzi, I thank you for your complete understanding of our devastating loss. I know that Abigail and Joby have somehow made us stronger. To Dave's sisters, I thank you for always remembering Joby in your own special ways. And to Joby's beloved BG, I thank you for always being there for us.

There were so many of you who helped my healing process along the way. All of our dear friends, I thank you. I thank all of you for being there for my family and me, and helping us in the creation and continuation of Joby's garden.

I want to make special acknowledgments of the following people who helped contribute to this book. First, I must thank my brother Dick Hahn, and my husband Dave, for painstakingly going over every edition of which there were many. Secondly, I thank Michael and Kate for listening to every draft I wrote even when they would have rather watched TV. I thank my sister Cheryl (Joby's godmother) who graciously donated her beautiful graphics for this book. I also extend my gratitude to Mr. Rich Stefanich, Mr. Chris Meeks, Cory Malchow, Staci Hamstra, and Star Swan. From the inspiration of Sally Downham Miller, Ph. D. and the guidance of Margaret Engleman, A.C.S.W.–B.C.D., I discovered the growth and healing that came from this writing.

Introduction

During one of the first family vacations after the death of our son, John Robert (Joby), I distinctly remember a moment that epitomizes the essence of losing a child. I was with my husband Dave, my daughter Kate, and my son Michael, along with Dave's sisters and their families. We were taking one of our traditional family vacations together. We were lying around a pool, somewhere out at sea on a family cruise. It was a beautiful sunny afternoon. Some of us were busy reading, others were listening to CD's through their earphones, and some were sharing jokes and telling stories.

    I was exhausted and tried to relax and soak up the warm rays of the sun. My personal grief had taken its toll, and it was all I could do to just be there. However, every time I closed my eyes, I saw Joby's beautiful face as clear as a bell. It was as if he were staring at me and smiling. I sat up quickly. I tried to jolt the image from my mind because it was too hard to bear. I didn't want to cry out loud in front of everyone.

    As I struggled to contain my tears, I spotted some muscular young boys walking around the pool. They were about Joby's age when he died. Then I surveyed the shallow end of the pool, and I saw some young boys playing. There was a young boy who specifically caught my eye. He had blonde hair, blue eyes, and skinny arms and legs. He was laughing and having a great time. He resembled every characteristic of my son when he was that young age. Odd, how I noticed every detail of every male child around me, and it was haunting.

    The grief began to swell within me. I rolled over on

my stomach, buried my face in my towel, and quietly wept. I could still hear everyone laughing and telling jokes, and all I could do was think about how unfair life had been. My oldest child wasn't here to enjoy any of this, and no one seemed to notice my pain. Instead, I felt alone in my grief, and realized how everyone else was moving on with their daily lives. I longed for the day when my life would be normal again. I battled the grief, the anger, and the resentment.

It would be moments like these that filled my life after losing my son. During those first few years after Joby's death, images of him, and the pain these images brought didn't disappear, but they did slowly lessen in intensity and in duration.

Through the years, I have been forced to realize that this horrible void was something that I would have to live with and make some sense out of. I battled with this empty feeling, whether I was alone or in the company of family and friends. This has been the most difficult struggle of my life. However, it is one that has also strengthened me over the years.

I believe that most of us who have been robbed of the joy of watching our children mature and grow into adulthood come to accept death as another stage of life. The horror of losing a child goes beyond any religion, race, or creed. This kind of pain is the same for everyone.

The inevitability of death awaits us all; however, losing a child has made me examine my faith and my beliefs. I do believe that there is an existence after this worldly life. It is not an existence that we physically understand; it is one of spiritual growth and communication. I don't believe a loving God takes our children from us. I don't believe any sins of the parents are visited upon the children. I don't believe that these tragedies are forms of punishment. We cannot blame God or a "Higher Being" for our misfortune.

I do believe, however, in bad luck and that sometimes "bad things do happen to good people."

From my strict Lutheran background, I have come to believe there is an afterlife. My faith has been challenged and altered in many ways since the death of my child. However, I still believe my son is in existence beyond this one, and I will join him one day. No matter what our faith is (whether it is one in God, a faith and love for our fellowman, or faith in some "Higher Power") I think much of the personal strength needed to tackle this grief will be drawn from our faith.

I hope that my recorded personal story of growth and healing can help you, the reader, to relate, understand, and possibly find new direction in your life. Remember, that friends and family can be a great help immediately upon the death of a child, but as time passes they have to go with their own lives and may not realize that you are stuck with this all consuming grief. I also discovered that people may try to simplify your pain, but it is far more complex than anyone realizes unless they have lost a child. It is also important to understand this grief process because while we may not be able to control what happens in our lives, we can control the way we react to tragedies. A parent who loses a child cannot continue living a life of "Why me?" or "Why did this happen to my child?" I believe we must all try to create a "different" life: one that is stronger—one that is wiser—and one that continues to develop personal growth and the ability to help others.

Joby Age One

Getting Started

Getting Started

Two days before his burial, we began our son's garden. My husband and I had our son cremated and buried behind our house so we could have him close to us. He was killed when he was only 16.

Dear friends were quick to help clear our land for the garden. They helped plant the flowers and trees, install the fish pond, hang the many bird feeders, place the donated statues and stepping stones, and place large rocks from our farm around the area. It was important for my husband and me to physically bury our child. It was our belief that we brought this child into this world, and we would lay him to bed one last time by our own hands. I realize now that this garden and the actual burying of our son marked the first day of healing in the process dealing with grief. The garden began taking on a life of its own and became the first testimonial to our son's life.

It was from the garden that the ideas for this writing grew. I began pounding away on the word processor. I cut through the layers of emotions just as I cut away at the land in preparation for the garden. It is a challenge for me to keep the flowers, plants, and trees alive that so many have given us. This physical process of planting, weeding, and replanting was my mission and my therapy. I struggled to create a beautiful living memorial from my son's untimely death. At the time, I didn't realize that this garden would also initiate my thoughts of this book. As I reflect, it is almost as if the seeds of my flowers were becoming seeds of thought for my writing.

When my parents died, I wrote poetry. When my brother died, I wrote in my journal. The death of my child has been so unnatural that the pain is almost more than I can bear. At first, writing about my son's death only seemed to reinforce the reality of the situation. Yet, the more I wrote, the more I discovered that the writing of this book took me to a different level of this experience. I have come to realize that grief is part of life's journey.

There is no cure; there is no quick fix; there is no specific point in time when the wound will completely heal and life will return to "normal." There is no certain form of recovery because the process of this kind of grief is a continual one. I once read that losing a child is more like losing one's future. A child without parents has a name; a spouse who has lost a mate has a name, but a parent who loses a child is still a parent. The scar of my son's death will remind me of how I am continuing to grow.

I remember one day, during the first few months after Joby's death, a gentleman from town approached me in our local hardware store. He embraced me and said, "I am so sorry about the loss of your son. My daughter was killed in a car accident when she had just turned 21."

Understanding his pain all too well, I replied, "Oh, I am so sorry. I want to thank you for caring. But how do we do handle this? I mean, how can we carry on?"

He replied, "Life doesn't really get better; it just gets different." Those words have stuck with me. The sooner I began to believe this, the sooner I could start the journey of living with grief. My immediate response to my son's death was to say that I accepted it when I really hadn't; to act like I was okay when I really wasn't; to say I must go on when I really didn't want to. I tried to listen to my inner self; sometimes faintly, but there were too many tears. Even when family and friends seemed to go on with their own daily lives (which they will and have to do), I could not. I knew that one day I would have to admit to myself that my son was dead. I discovered that life wasn't getting better; it was very, very different.

The purpose of this book is to help another parent or family member or friend who has experienced the death of a child to endure those very tough first years after the loss. I have organized my own journey of growth and healing through the first three years after the death of my son. I discovered three basic steps to help those left behind to survive. The three basic steps are (1) "Taking Care of You and Yours," (2) "Relating to Others," and (3) "Taking Action." These three steps, no matter what stage of grief (and I discovered the stages of denial, anger, acceptance, growth and healing) or what year one might be experiencing, can hopefully help the reader better understand the process of grief.

July 20, 1997 (from my journal):

It's as if I am talking about someone else. I feel your presence within me and then a flashback of the phone call, seeing you lying there in the emergency room, cold, blue, liquid oozing from your mouth and nose, the tube sticking from your mouth. I held your hand, still a bit warm to the touch. I ran my hand through your hair, I kissed you all over your face. I tried to hold you but was afraid to pick you up—weird thoughts. I wanted to stay; Dad said we had to leave. How could I leave you? I wanted you home. Joby, I miss you. Everything seems like a charade, and all I want is you back again.

*Remembering the Day
Of My Son's Death*

Remembering the Day of My Son's Death

Sunday, May 18, 1997

Joby's death was a shock to everyone. In this small town of Rensselaer, Indiana, his untimely death was a cold reminder of our own mortality. In a small community, a teenager's death made headline news.

Remembering that day of May 18, 1997, is like re-living the nightmare in slow motion. The phone call, the drive to the hospital, the waiting in the emergency room until we heard news of our son's condition can all be replayed in my mind in detail.

It was the day after Prom, and my husband and I hadn't let our son, who was a sophomore, go to the big school event the night before. (We thought that he could wait until he was a junior or senior to attend Prom. Instead, we told Joby he could go to a scheduled birthday party at a friend's house the day after.) It was almost noon. I had bad feelings about this party because he told us they were going to ride a four wheeler. I remember arguing with Joby that I really didn't want him to go and told him to be home early. I hadn't been fond of the four wheelers since two high school students, who attended the same high school where I taught, had been killed while riding ATVs. My husband reassured me that Joby would be fine as he would talk to him about safety precautions. Shortly after Joby left, my husband Dave had to leave for work.

It was around three in the afternoon, and I had been on the phone trying to find a home for a stray dog that had come to our house. My husband came running into the house and told me he got a phone call at work that Joby had been in an accident. I quickly hung up the phone. Our daughter Kate was home with me, and I told her to stay put in case her brother Michael came back from playing neighborhood football. I reassured her that Joby was okay and probably had some minor injuries.

My husband and I rushed to the hospital under my repeated cautions to slow down. The thought that our son was hurt terribly was the furthest thought from my mind. I reminded him that we didn't want to kill ourselves just in getting there. However, once we reached the emergency area, we both sensed that something was dreadfully wrong, jumped out of the car and flew into the emergency room. I couldn't explain it then, but this time the trip to the emergency room at our local hospital seemed to hold more urgency than the other visits we had made to the E.R. As we entered, we saw our son's friends sitting there crying. Some were hysterical, holding their heads in their hands and holding one another. The pain was apparent in their faces. I quickly turned and asked someone, "Is Joby alive? Is he still alive?"

"Yes, yes," I heard, "but, Brenda, listen..." I don't remember exactly what she was telling me, but there had been an accident or something like that. I clung to the answer of "Yes" and forced myself to believe that my son, my 16 year old child, was still alive. There was hope. She continued to say something, and I believe I just nodded.

Dave, on the other hand, was demanding, "What happened?" over and over again. Joby's friends were trying to tell us about the accident. I heard something about a four-wheeler that collided with Joby as he was trying to jump out of the way. There is nothing to prepare a parent for that.

  Nothing was making sense to Dave or me. Dave paced; he shouted, "This doesn't look good, Brenda!" They still wouldn't let us in the emergency room; we were told that they were working on him and we couldn't see him. What did this mean?

  Feelings of confusion and panic began to permeate the room. Time stood still and we waited with the rest of them. I hugged Joby's friends and reassured them that their best friend was strong and that he would be all right. I was clinging to the hope that my son was still alive.

  Dave and I were finally ushered into an isolated emergency room…and we waited again. The ambulance driver popped in only to comment to Dave, "It didn't look good." What did that mean? I thought. Was Joby paralyzed, more broken bones than I imagined, internal injuries? What did this all mean? My husband paced alongside the emergency room bed and shook his head, muttering. In total shock and confusion, I stood near the door in front of the bed.

  It seemed like an eternity before the doctor came in and directed her comments to my husband, bypassing me who was standing next to her as she entered the room. "Dave, I'm sorry…we couldn't save him…" and then I think she said something else. Dave turned and hit the wall and moaned in pain; I remember falling to my knees in a dry cry.

  I immediately got up and pushed the question, "Why aren't you in there doing something? I want to see him! I want to see him now!"

They told me we had to wait again...that they had to clean him up. I was furious; I was shocked; I felt helpless.

From an essay by Cory Malchow (a friend of Joby's):

...The date was May 18, 1997. I should know; it was my birthday...When I got closer and closer I noticed that the one-ton truck magically changed into an ambulance. I was wondering what the heck was going on here. Despair and worries went through my head. When I pulled into the drive, I noticed Sean was sprinkled in blood. His hands were on top of his forehead and he kept repeating, 'Oh, my God, what have I done?' Ambyr and Alina were crying together, with some stuttering. Tab tried to explain to me what had happened. Joby was on the ground, still, motionless, almost as if there was no more soul in his body to let him move with ease.

His hands and face already black, blue, and purple, kind of like a movie, but happening in real life. I wish it was a movie, but in the movies if you die you live for another movie to act in. As Tab told me the story, I could imagine the movement of Joby's feet and hands when he got into the accident...

"...Sean had the four wheeler and Joby had the ezee-go electric golf-cart. Joby decided to put the ezee-go electric golf cart away into

the garage and wanted to talk to Sean. Sean was over by the road heading toward the house.

Sean saw Joby and headed toward him…Sean got close enough to Joby, that Joby bolted to the right, but Sean bolted to the left, causing a collision with both of them. Joby did a flip in the air and hit the ground head first, causing his neck to snap instantly. Sean got a black eye from Joby as he was in the air. After the collision Sean immediately jumped off the four-wheeler to attend his dead friend on the ground, leaving the four-wheeler to crash into the ditch…How I wish I could have helped him, but there was nothing I could have done. Just sit there and stare at the paramedics working on him…

As a mother, I wanted to see and experience everything my son had endured immediately before his death. I had to know; I had to feel his pain. I was there with him through life and wanted so desperately to be with him through death. It was so unfair. He lay there as if in a morbid sleep. I never saw Joby sleeping on his back so straight; he was a scruncher; he would curl up in a ball. I wanted to move him onto his side; to caress and hold him, but a quick fear went through my mind that if I moved him, I might hurt him.

How ridiculous this must sound, but when you see your child lying there lifeless, nothing much makes sense anymore. David rushed to his side, sobbing Joby's name. I followed. Dave stood on one side of the bed, and I on the other. We still never comforted one another...we were both frozen in our own pain and we both moaned, "Oh, my, God, no!! Oh, Joby, Joby, our sweet Joby!"

He was already bluish. That surprised me; he must have died earlier than we thought. His hair was still in place; his eyes were shut; his hands were the one thing I held because they were still warm to the touch. I wanted to stay there...just sit there with him, holding his hand. I stroked his hair, kissed his face all over, and held him the best I could as he just lay there. An emergency attendant began to tell us that Joby had broken his pelvis and went on to say "See, look; his diaphragm must have also exploded. See how inflamed his chest and stomach are..." I thought to myself why doesn't he just shut up! I couldn't believe he could refer to Joby as a medical class example; this was our son.

He finally left.

I opened one of my son's eyes; I had to see those blue, blue eyes just one more time. I gently caressed his shoulders and arms. I just couldn't let go.

Our other two children were brought to the hospital, not knowing that their brother was dead. Kate brought my purse, thinking I might need it. I didn't even know at the time how they got there, but there they were outside Joby's door. Dave and I went out and told them that Joby had died and that they might want to go in the room and say good-bye. The four of us made a group hug. Then Michael, who was only 19 months younger than his brother, entered first, but almost immediately came flying out of the room and raced down the hall. I saw our good friends Estel George and Jim Anderson run after Michael to be with him. We were lucky to have close friends near us since neither Dave nor I have family members who live near our town.

Kate and I, holding each other's hand, entered the room. I think I said something about how Joby looked peaceful, almost as if he were sleeping. She and I stood there stroking his hand and holding it. Then our friends began to come in, the minister, and more people. Everyone was drifting in and out; yet the moment was frozen in time for me.

The week following his death would drag on for an eternity. We had his "showing" at our church, the student-packed funeral at the high school, the preparation of the garden, the private family burial at our house, and the memorial ceremony by his golf team.

From the eulogy by Rich Stefanich (Joby's golf coach):

...in closing, let's remember that smile, that competitiveness, the striving for academic success, that friendliness, that concern for doing the 'right thing' that characterized Joby. Let's keep his memory alive by trying, as students and friends, to emulate those characteristics that have impacted so many of us.

I can recount details about the actual day of his death, but the days later were a blur. I cannot forget the daily pain and the daily crying I experienced that first year after his death. I would have died a thousand deaths to have my son back.

July 27, 1997 (from my journal):

Come back to us, sweet son, in the warmth of our arms so diligently we guarded you. You aren't allowed to be taken from us this quickly.
It's just not supposed to happen this way...

The First Year After His Death

The First Year After His Death

It was a year of shock, denial, and desperate attempts to connect in some way to our child with whom we had no time to say our good-byes. I found him in my dreams; I thought I heard his voice; things happened around the house that were inexplicable. During that first year, there were so many signs of Joby that I believe I didn't catch them all. After reading several books, I began to realize these possibly weren't signs "of" my son but rather signs "from" him. I say this hesitantly because I know people, including myself, are very skeptical about the subject of spirituality and life beyond the one of this earth.

Strange coincidences happened after Joby's death. For instance, about a month after Joby was killed, I found myself getting my family ready for an already scheduled family vacation. I had been going through Joby's things with my son Michael to see if he wanted a T-shirt or something of his brother's. We went through some of his things until Michael needed a break, and before I could shut Joby's dresser drawer, I spotted an old raggedy red tank shirt.

I had never seen it in Joby's things before and asked Michael where his brother got it. Mike replied, "Oh, he took it out of Dad's stuff a while back." Not thinking much about it, I took the red tank top and put it back in my husband's things. That night I had the most vivid dream of Joby. It was a sweet dream where he came downstairs early one morning while I was preparing pancakes. He came into the kitchen and told me he loved me and kissed me on the cheek. That dream carried me through the night.

The next day, Joby's girlfriend Staci Hamstra came over to say good-bye to us before we left for our trip. She had come over often that first year and that was a blessing. We sat down to chat for a while and before she left, she began to tell me of her first dream of Joby that she had the night before. I told her ironically that I had my first dream of him also last night, but I waited to hear her story first.

She began to tell me that the dream took place at school. Although Joby was there, nobody could see him but her. She asked him why he was there, and he told her he was going to say good-bye to his family but Kate had already left. "My, God, Kate did leave last Sunday with her grandmother, and we are going to meet them this weekend!" I commented.

Then she went on to say, "Well, I thought the weird part of the dream was that he was wearing a red tank top that I had never seen him wear before!" I just sat there in amazement and began to explain to her the entire events that had taken place just the day before in Joby's bedroom.

The first year was full of coincidences like the one above. Joby's favorite songs would pop on the radio when some of us were thinking about or speaking about him. Once, during the middle of one of Michael's wrestling tournaments, I was reading a book and came across a passage by Elisabeth Kubler-Ross who had likened "death to a cocoon metamorphosing into a butterfly." I leaned back on the bleachers and thought to myself how lovely an image. As I was doing this, I happened to rub my right ear and noticed that I had worn the last pair of earrings that my son Joby had gotten for me just two days before his last birthday. Those earrings were a pair of small butterflies.

Another incident occurred shortly after the funeral when family members were beginning to return to their homes. This particular story concerns one of my sisters, Cheryl, who was Joby's godmother. In the last few years of Joby's life, his interest in art began to grow. For his last birthday, I had given him a sketch book and drawing pencils. Before my sister left for home, I decided she should have Joby's sketch book since she was a professional artist. When she returned home to the state of Washington, she gave me a call. She informed me that she looked through the book to find only a couple of sketches but that the last drawing that he had been working on happened to match her latest piece of artwork. Even though we had never seen her artwork or visited her art studio, the abstract drawing was almost identical to hers except for the colors he had used.

Another incident occurred to a classmate and teammate of Joby's who wrote me a letter after the funeral. Star Swan was a senior at the time and a fellow golfer. She and Joby happened to have the same make of car, a silver Fiero. Since Joby was too young to drive his car, Star would take Joby to and from practice after school.

She told me that he would always joke with her. He would tell her how his car was in better condition and drove better, all the while playing and tugging at a thumb tack she had used to keep the inside roof lining of her car in place. While she was driving home from the funeral,

"American Pie" (Joby's favorite song and one we played at the funeral) came on over the radio. She began to cry and talk to Joby. Suddenly, that same thumb tack that Joby would always fiddle with came flying out of the ceiling of the car and landed on her arm. She told me she almost drove off the road. It was almost as if Joby were joking with her for one last time. Months would follow with such coincidental occurrences happening to different friends and family members.

I was beginning to think that maybe Joby was communicating to many of us. Although some people still denied the possibility that this could actually be happening, all I can say is that it did. When I stopped questioning these occurrences so much, they came as a blessing not just a coincidence.

June 1997 (from my journal):

I heard Mom, Mom...Mommy...
Joby's voice!
Was it really him?
I've had dreams—encounters of Joby's presence; doors open, his word processor clicked on in the middle of the night...

The arrival of the first winter was an extremely painful process for the garden and me. When the first snow fell, I was extremely anxious. I initially thought that the blanket of snow would be a symbolic blanket of comfort over my son. Much to my surprise it became a cold, suffocating cover over his grave.

Each morning I would get up early and dust off the

snow that covered his grave. It seems crazy now, but each time it snowed, I hated it and felt that it was as if nature was mocking his death and trying to cover it up. I hated that first winter of cold and ice and snow.

It was also a time of holidays, and I found it difficult to feign cheer or happiness. No one seemed to understand, but it was impossible for me to be joyful no matter how much other family members tried or wanted me to be.

Spring finally arrived, and the bulbs I had planted in the fall began to appear. Nature was growing as it should. I bought more items for his garden and displayed the memorabilia with pride. Joby's garden sits directly behind our home. It is a free flowing garden that stretches approximately 150 feet by 20 feet with several Hawthorn trees that outline its curved s-shape. His grave stone sits in the middle of the garden under one of the Hawthorns. There are tall purple irises that tower behind his large engraved stone, purple sage and a bleeding heart plant to the left of his grave site, a small donated Thunder Child tree and a small pond to the right. His school's baseball team donated their winning "no hit" ball for the garden which we had encased in a weather-proof, plexi-glass stand that sits off to the right of this rock. Behind the garden is an acre of wildflowers and then a dense woods which heightens the beauty of the garden plantings. I added more plants including donated lilac and butterfly bushes, yellow and purple cone flowers, three wisterias, and numerous ferns and hostas. The garden and the care it required slowly began to bring me out of the depths of a winter long depression. May was approaching. My garden and I were about to make it through that first year.

September 12, 1997 (from my journal):

The emptiness, the pain it strikes with such force. I gasp for breath.
Will I breathe again?
Can I live again?
You are such a part of me.
I just can't let go.

❑ ❑ ❑ ❑

STEP ONE: Taking Care of You and Yours:

I refer to this first step as "Taking Care of You and Yours"—it is with this first step that I learned to help my immediate family and myself through the daily routine of life. Each day seemed to drag on like a slow nightmare for each of us. We found it physically and emotionally painful to wake–up each morning. It was as if we carried this constant, suffocating feeling making even breathing difficult. We discovered grieving to be extremely exhausting.

I found the physical touch very comforting, and the need for it seemed greater that first year. I tried to give daily hugs to my husband and children. Days and weeks passed, and I had no idea what I did or how I survived. The "knife–cutting" and "gut wrenching" feeling was there on a daily basis that first year, and crying was sometimes uncontrollable.

I quickly discovered that each of us in my immediate family was experiencing the grieving process in different ways. It became a time of recognizing feelings and pain that my husband, my other two children, and I never knew existed. We were all embarking upon a journey of grief that would be different for each of us. We couldn't change what had happened; "bad things do happen to good people!"

During this time, it was easy to fall into binges one way or another. I tried to drink less caffeine; it wickedly kept me up through awful nights. I tried not to mask the pain with drugs and alcohol. I hesitate to even mention this, because I know that certain anti–depressants or anti–anxiety medication can be helpful. However, I saw how easy it was to over–indulge and try to mask the reality of what had happened. For me, I had to be careful not to try and "drink" away my pain.

That first year was a time of paradoxes. It was a time I had to do whatever was needed in order for my family and me to survive. I tried to positively nurture my body and mind in order to be strong, not only for my family but also for myself.

I do think it is very important for a husband and wife to be there for each other and to help one another be strong for the other children. That first year, my husband and I had to return to work immediately after Joby's death, yet we were always on call for one another. We made a pact that if one of us ever needed the other, no questions asked, we would be there.

I gave up trying to be "wonder woman" or "super mom." I did what I could do, and I tried not to set any of us on a timetable for grieving. Because I have other children, I also thought it was imperative that my husband and I try to demonstrate to our children healthy ways to express grief.

I was a high school teacher and being able to come

home when my husband was "having a bad day" was sometimes difficult, but I did it. Dave owns and manages his own furniture business, so he made it a point to always be there for me. Priorities had to be made. We had to be stronger than we ever thought we possibly could be.

We left little notes to one another expressing our love. I also wrote letters to my children letting them know how much we loved them and needed them. I tried to recognize their own strength in the way they had handled themselves after losing their brother. I had to let them know how proud I was of them. Siblings tend to get lost in the grief of the parents, and I believe it was vital that I recognized their pain. The loss of their brother was just as real for them as it was for my husband and me.

I remember the first few nights after Joby was killed, Michael and Kate felt alone and isolated. Even though they had many friends who came over to the house, much of the attention by friends was given to us, the parents. As shocked as we still were, Michael and Kate were equally shocked and fearful. Michael was only an eighth grader and Kate was a fifth grader at the time. Joby, Michael, and Kate were very close siblings and did everything together. So, we let Kate and Mike grab their sleeping bags and pick a sleeping place in our bedroom. It helped all of us to talk and pray together those first few nights.

During that first year, I was advised to write in my journal more. I tried but I couldn't. Sometimes I wrote about feelings, but I usually wrote about what we were doing. Writing was not a solace at that time for me; however, I know several mothers who found the writing very helpful immediately after the loss of a child.

During that first year, there were more "firsts" for Kate and Michael. Kate had to start middle school as a sixth grader. Sometimes facing so many of her friends so soon after her brother's death was awkward for her. Yet, the new school probably helped her in some ways so that she could busy herself with "new" things.

Michael had to start high school without his older brother and that was another difficult adjustment. There were reminders of his brother everywhere at school. All of Joby's friends were there, and I know that was hard on Michael. I think, at times, he resented their presence because his brother was not there. However, Joby's friends were quick to try to fill in the gaps for Mike, and he has since developed strong friendships with them.

Probably one of the toughest adjustments for Michael was when he wrestled on the junior varsity team, and occasionally he would wrestle varsity that first year. This is the one sport both brothers did together. (Joby had been active in tennis, basketball, wrestling, and golf. Michael's talents led him to football, wrestling and sometimes baseball and cross-country. The wrestling, however, had always been a shared activity between the boys since they started AAU wrestling when they were very young.) Joby would have been on the varsity team that year and the varsity team wore their green ribbons in memory of him. It was a proud moment to see those wrestlers with their green ribbons pinned to their warm-up jackets, but it was also an emotional one as well.

Even for Dave and me, going into that high school for athletic events or parent-teacher conferences for Michael were awkward moments. There seemed to linger that pain of emptiness that was felt every time we went there. Walking by Joby's locker was painful for me. Everything looked different now to us and it seemed people were treating us differently. It all just seemed more intense now. That first year would be adjustments for all of us in different ways. We were all in shock that first year. Reality of Joby's loss had not sunken in yet.

I think Step One of "Taking Care of You and Yours" helped me evaluate what I could handle emotionally and physically as well as what my husband and children needed from me. I recognized the need for hugs, letters of support, patience, and understanding from all of us. I tried not to feel guilty for so many unexplained emotions. I learned to recognize the different ways in which my own family members were dealing with the process of grief, no matter how confusing it was. But, it all was a very exhausting process.

❑ ❑ ❑ ❑

STEP TWO: Relating to Others:

I refer to the second step as "Relating to Others." Step Two concerns learning more about my relationships with others, outside the nuclear family. I tried not to be offended by others who wanted to put me on a time limit for grief. The stages of grief are endured differently by each individual. I discovered that family members and dear friends were quick to advise, but we had to try and keep in mind that they couldn't possibly understand the devastation of such a loss unless they had lost a child.

Six months after my son's death, I distinctly remember a colleague at work saying to me, "You know,

Brenda, bad things happen to a lot of people; I lost my grandmother just recently. You need to move on." I broke into tears and challenged his sense of understanding. Losing a grandmother or even a parent didn't compare to the feeling I was experiencing after losing a child. I even had family members tell me that I needed to "move on" for the sake of my own family. I was so angry that I couldn't speak.

I came to realize that what people said many times simply reflected a lack of understanding. I tried to keep this in perspective and realize that most people were only trying to help. I had to remember that my pain was probably awkward for them. I believe most of these people wanted to help but just didn't know exactly what to say or know what to do.

However, many friends and family were there for us that critical first year after our son's death. A dear colleague at school who taught a few doors down the hallway from my classroom would drop an encouraging note in my mailbox every week. At first, I was deeply surprised to receive such comfort. Then as time passed, I looked forward to receiving her notes. Her continual acts of kindness made me feel less alone, especially at work. Many of our friends would continue to make phone calls and offer to help in any way with Kate and Michael, and I would receive monthly mail from my sisters. I even had a friend from our old neighborhood who made a point to visit Joby's garden and leave flowers and a note on his grave on special occasions. I would find these gifts every time I returned home from work. They were a comfort and a blessing that someone remembered. It is important to remember those who are in grief, especially after the funeral and after everyone leaves. Months into that first year of grieving is a time when friends and family can so easily forget the needs of those left behind.

This was also a time that I was flooded with visits by Joby's friends, and I thrived on these meetings. Either a group of girls or a group of his male friends would drop by and talk. We would share stories of Joby and I treasured these moments of reminiscing. Even his teachers would stop by periodically which meant a great deal to me. One teacher in particular was Joby's first art teacher, Bill Roeschlein, from the middle school. He and Joby had a wonderful teacher/student relationship that cultivated into a lasting friendship. In fact that first year, Mr. Roeschlein came to visit the garden right before Christmas time. He brought some of Joby's friends and they came and placed a beautiful holiday grave blanket on his grave sight. In turn, we shared stories and remembered Joby.

Mr. Roeschlein continues to remember us around this difficult holiday and brings his traditional winter grave blanket with him for the garden. These visits help all of us in different ways.

Unfortunately, not all get–togethers with other people were fulfilling for me because I didn't feel I could talk about Joby in the way I could when I was with his close friends. Family trips were now a difficult time for me, but Dave and I felt our children needed the physical change at the time. Both Michael and Kate enjoy our families which are rather large. Dave is the oldest of four and I am the youngest of seven children. When we get together with either family, it becomes a major event.

At that point, I only wanted to be alone with my

own immediate family and trying to relate to extended families was too much of a major task. After Joby's death, I was a zombie through that first vacation with Dave's sisters and their families. Every time we went out, I just counted. I counted only four chairs around our restaurant table instead of five; I counted the number of children in other families; I counted one less child at every family function. I noticed every blue-eyed blonde boy and thought it was Joby. I was often asked that dreaded question by people we would meet, "So how many children do you have?" How awkward that simple question was now. How could I respond without dishonoring the memory of my dead child? All in all, I was miserable.

We were in beautiful country in the Grand Tetons, Yellowstone Park, and Glacier National Park, but I couldn't see the beauty of it all because everywhere I looked, I only saw that Joby was not with us. Though we tried our best to enjoy what we could, Dave and I had many strained moments. All of us were emotionally exhausted when we returned home.

As I look back, maybe we shouldn't have gone on that trip. Yet, at the time, I think Dave and I were trying to keep things as normal for our children as possible. We did discover that "normalcy" was relative, and our lives were very different now. I tried to remind myself that "different" didn't have to be bad, and it could offer an opportunity for growth for the entire family but this was difficult to accept at this early stage of grief.

When the first holidays approached without our son, they were unspeakable. I asked myself: "How can I be thankful at a time when my child is gone?" For our family, Thanksgiving has been traditionally held at my husband's Uncle John's farm in Kentucky. Dave and I made the decision to attend even though this was just months after losing Joby. We hoped that staying together as a family would give all of a sense of continuity in this rocky time. It also became a time that allowed our family members to witness just how difficult this process was for us. They, too, learned from this experience.

Christmas was especially difficult for my immediate family. "Do we hang up Joby's Christmas stocking or not?" "Should we even have a Christmas tree this first year?" Listening to Christmas carols and decorating the house were added reminders of our loss. It wasn't easy trying to decorate as usual when things were far from normal. Hanging Joby's stocking up (as I still do) right along with the rest of ours became a heart–wrenching ordeal.

Christmas Eve and Christmas Day were traditionally spent at my sister Carol's home in Danville, Indiana, with the rest of my family. It was not an easy time. Nevertheless, my husband and I felt the need to stay with the family ties once again. It was important not to slip into that painful pit of despair.

I think we all tried to be strong emotionally, but it was an awkward time for us because we did not know exactly what to do or how to act around one another. We all knew we were hurting and missed Joby, and we didn't want to make matters worse. Even though this first year was filled with mostly denial, I can recall an early "anger episode" that happened between my son Michael and me.

It occurred a few days after Christmas when Michael, Kate, and I were taking down our tree. All of the decorations and lights were off by now because none of us could really fake any sense of celebration during this season. Though each of us had been silently dealing with our pain, this silence abruptly ended when Michael and I were tying to maneuver the tree out the living room door and out to our back deck.

I don't remember exactly what triggered the incident, but I uncharacteristically lashed out at him. I screamed some verbal obscenity, and he returned the remark. We both just stared at each other with tears in our eyes. It frightened both of us, including poor Kate who was standing off to the side. In tears, Michael dropped his end of the tree and ran out the door. Immediately, I dropped my end of the Douglas Fir and went chasing after him.

I ran right up to him, crying and begging him to forgive me. We cried together and embraced. We stood there holding one another. The entire incident scared us both so much that we vowed never to allow this to happen again.

What I learned was that sometimes unspoken anger over the death of a child can erupt without warning during unrelated situations. I also soon learned that my anger over Joby's death could get misconstrued by my other children. We all knew we had a long way to go in this journey of grief.

This Step of "Relating to Others" also included our need to make connections with "others" who had lost a child. I was surprised to discover just how many grieving parents there were in our community. Many of these parents had already contacted us after the death of our son, and these connections became one of our strongest support systems. My husband and I became very close to a few couples we had met at a Compassionate Friends meeting. These Compassionate Friends meetings were held in Lafayette just about 40 minutes south of where we lived. These meetings consisted of parents who had lost children, and they would gather in a circle and share their stories. It was also a time in which we could ask questions to other parents and gain a true perspective and understanding from others who experienced similar losses. One of the mothers whom I met had lost her only daughter about a month after my son's death. She and I have become dear friends and check–in on each other from time to time. We have learned a great deal from each other's journey. Even though she remains active in Compassionate Friends and I have chosen another path, we share a unique and lasting bond. She always reminds me how lucky we were to have had such wonderful children.

At first, when I listened to other grieving parents, I must admit that I would think that they couldn't possibly have loved their child as much I loved my son. "Oh, no, my situation was different; my child was killed; my child was a good student; my child was well liked; my child had such a promising career. I missed him more than any of these other parents!" How foolish I was to think these things, but that was exactly how I felt. What I have learned is that every parent misses his or her child to the same degree as I did. It became evident that as parents, we all love our children unconditionally and no matter how the child was taken, or no matter how old the child was; we all grieve. We all feel that pain. That was the first lesson I learned from these parents.

I also discovered that we were all crying out to tell "our story," and we needed an understanding ear. It was helpful for me that I could openly express my pain to people who understood. These other parents who were enduring similar situations were extremely supportive. By talking with them, I was able to validate my own feelings, and I knew I was not alone. The parents who had survived the first or second or third year after their child's death were invaluable to us also. They taught us that there was some visible "light" at the far side of this experience.

Step Two ("Relating to Others") was a challenge and a reward at the same time. I gradually learned to accept comments from others without being judgmental, and, in turn, I learned more about myself.

July 21, 1997 (from my journal):

...So many people, but nothing seems important to me. I just wanted my son here. Don't they understand? Can't they see the pain is too great?

☐ ☐ ☐ ☐

STEP THREE: Taking Action:

Step Three was about taking physical action to express the grief, and for that reason I refer to this step as "Taking Action." The first year I found that I was extremely active in memorializing my son. Perhaps, I became obsessed with having to do something. I felt I needed this physical approach so I could work out and sort through all these myriad of emotions flooding my mind on a daily basis. I would come to realize the importance of physically doing something and keeping active were essential in handling the grief process in a healthy, constructive way.

Since we cremated Joby and buried his ashes in the back yard, the memory garden was the most satisfying action step I took. The idea of growing plants, trees, and flowers in our son's memory was, and still is, extremely therapeutic for me.

However, one of the first action steps of dealing with grief was made by my son's friends during the wake. Joby's wake was held at our church. At first, the idea of "displaying" his body was repulsive to me, and I didn't want it. However, it was advised to us that especially when someone young dies, a physical showing, when possible, helps the friends deal with the death and allows them to say their good–byes. Students and friends filed continually throughout the afternoon and in to the night. I somehow gained emotional strength for the students who were there, and I believe their presence helped me get through this highly emotional event.

During the wake, I remember vividly when Joby's golf team was led in by one of his friends and pallbearers Alex Abel. I noticed they were all wearing green ribbons on their lapels. I approached Alex and as he handed me several green ribbons, he said, "Mrs. Greene, we want you and your family to have these. We are wearing these in memory of Joby." Our family and his friends wore those ribbons for the entire first year after his death. Those green ribbons became a unity symbol for all of Joby's friends and my family. We were proud to wear them, and they allowed us to freely talk about him. I think one of a parent's greatest fears is that people will forget his of her child. Therefore, these ribbons were ways in which we kept his memory alive.

Many more "action" steps were taken by the students at Joby's school.

The high school administration at that time was extremely empathic and allowed the students to cope with this sudden death of their classmate and friend. Joby was killed on a Sunday afternoon, and on Monday the students were allowed to mourn and write letters of their memories of Joby for the first two hours of school. I was given a basket of these messages the next day. The school flew the flag outside the building at half-mast and called in ministers to counsel with the students.

I have taught in many school corporations where they did little or nothing when a student died. As a teacher and a parent, I was impressed with the way in which Rensselaer Central High School handled the situation. Although Rensselaer is a small town of only about 5,000 people, the immediate comfort that we received was overwhelming and memorable.

Joby's funeral, I believe, was one of the first major steps of healing for his classmates. It was held in the auditorium of his high school where an estimated 1,500 people were in attendance. Music, something Joby loved, was a major emphasis. We played some of his favorite songs, ranging from "Tears in Heaven" by Eric Clapton, "American Pie" by Don McLean to "It's a Wonderful World" by Louis Armstrong. The school choir also dedicated two songs to him. The music was played before, during, and after the ceremony and it seemed to help all of us through this emotional time. Students, teachers, and family (including Dave and me) spoke about their memories of Joby and said their good-byes.

My poem I read at the funeral:

Our Dearest Joby,
I look at the sunset and
I see the warm glow in your eyes.
The breeze softly touches my cheek,
as I feel your strong arms around me.
I see the array of colorful flowers
placed so delicately around the rocks,
and I know you will be pleased
to be a part of this earth that you so greatly
loved.
You touched us all.
We are blessed by your existence
which is not measured by the time within the
hour glass,
but rather, measured by the greatness
and the love of your goodness.
I see the twinkle in your beautiful blue eyes,
the laughter of your sweet smile, and the softness of your hair.
I wrap them up in my heart forever.
For I know you are 'God's Special Angel'.

An upperclassman Ryan Brown was instrumental in presenting a slide show of Joby's life. Joby's sophomore class attended as a group. At the end of the service, they paraded by us placing a rose in a basket for us. I saved those roses until the first anniversary of his death and, at that time, sprinkled the rose petals over his grave. With the death of someone so young, I believe it was important to plan a funeral that allowed "actions" of grief for both family and friends of Joby.

> **From a eulogy given by one of Joby's close friends:**
>
> *Hello, my name is Cory Malchow, and I have a story to tell about Joby and Sean, who were best friends. An hour before the accident, Joby and Sean were talking about the things they wanted to do before they died. They both agreed that they wanted to go skydiving. Since Joby can't jump out of an airplane, today I promise to go skydiving for him....*

Another example of Step Three was a result of an unusual occurrence during the burial of our son. As I have already discussed the irony of my butterfly earrings that related so poignantly to a passage in Elizabeth Kubler-Ross' book about the stages of grief, I would also like to share with the reader why butterfly pins have been my symbol for Joby. The idea came about when my brother-in-law Mark was playing his guitar at the private burial at our house. Mark was in the middle of the song "For Bobby" by John Denver and had just completed the lyrics "...and the wind will whisper your name to me." At that moment, a gust of wind rushed across all of us, almost causing Mark's sheet music to fall, and it crossed over the garden. I immediately smiled and stared at everyone who shared in the "eerie" feeling. I then turned and looked straight at Joby's grave stone where I saw a tiny monarch perched on the rock. I still give butterfly pins to friends for inspiration and hope when they are confronted with their own personal tragedy.

When we buried his ashes, Dave, Mike, Kate, and I also added a sentimental item, our last family photo, and Joby's friends' notes and mementos. By doing this we were able to say good-bye in a demonstrative way.

A few days after the funeral, Joby's friends demonstrated more ways to express their grief. His golf teammates created a beautiful memorial at the town's Curtis Creek Golf Course. This was where they practiced each day and where Joby had experienced his first summer job. A small memorial ceremony was held at the golf course. The team presented a memorial tree and plaque while the golf pro (also an accomplished vocalist) sang a beautiful operatic song in dedication to Joby.

> **From the eulogy by Rich Stefanich (Joby's golf coach):**
>
> *Joby was the product of such a happy, secure, loving family. This showed in his demeanor and his attitude toward his friends, school, and athletics. Perhaps the greatest manifestation of this was his smile—I always enjoyed that—as a teacher and coach. That smile really shined when he achieved a good grade in my class—and, happily, I saw it often there...I loved that smile on the golf course...*

At the end of that school year, his wrestling team dedicated their highlight tape to their teammate Joby, and the school yearbook staff rushed a one-page insert for publication in dedication to their classmate. Our ability to make this transition of change was made easier because of our school and our community's constant acts of support.

From the eulogy by Chris Meeks (Joby's wrestling coach):

After the season was finished, I would see Joby every once in a while in the hallways or locker room. I would ask him how his brother Michael was doing in middle school wrestling and his face would light up, bragging how good of a wrestler Michael was and could be. It was very obvious that Joby was extremely proud of his little brother. I also knew Joby was really looking forward to being on the same team with Michael next year. In fact, his father was working on putting together a weight room downstairs in their house for the two boys to train together this summer.

Monday, I met after school with the wrestling team and we talked about Joby for a while. I told the kids I was going to deliver this eulogy and wanted to share some of them with you. The following are some of their comments describing their teammate: 'Competitor,' 'Aggressive,' 'Go–getter,' 'Always gave 100%... 'A true teammate,' and 'A friend.' It has been said that teachers and coaches make an impact on their students and athletes' lives. Let it also be said that these same students and athletes also make an impact on their teachers' and coaches' lives, too. Joby Greene has made a lasting impression on my life, his teammates, and, I'm sure, yours, too.

Joby's friends also created a "clubhouse" or meeting place in his honor. It was named "The Greene Room." Initially, it was created as a place to help one another through their loss and to memorialize their friend. One of Joby's pallbearers and good friends offered the room above his parents' garage. This project was healthy for the kids to actively pull together and help one another. Chairs, lamps, rugs, TV's, video games, etc., were all donated by families and "The Greene Room" began to take shape. This meeting place would serve these teens for the next few years.

At the end of the school year, I was given Joby's school records by the guidance counselor. The school counselor at the time (Linda Anderson) was a good friend of mine, and she knew Joby very well. She took it upon herself to gather all of his records and gave them to me. I then asked teachers for any videos, artwork, or any projects of his that they still had. I would never have thought of asking for these materials had it not been for Linda, and I was grateful. All of these forms of documentation helped in their own way.

Within a month, Dave and I initiated a scholarship in Joby's name at his high school. The school was extremely receptive. Our son was a good student, and he enjoyed sports. His scholarship would honor students of athletic ability, high academic standards, and positive mental attitude. The scholarship was one of the first efforts we made to demonstrate our appreciation for the school's overwhelming support.

During that first Christmas, we took an action that helped the immediate family immeasurably. We purchased a puppy on Michael's 15th birthday, December 22, 1997. We certainly didn't need another dog as we had two already, but that new puppy helped us get through that holiday. It helped us take our minds off of our loss and concentrate on this new little life form that had now become a new member of our family.

It was also during this first Christmas I began a project at home. I displayed many of Joby's school pictures, awards, certificates, etc. on a basement wall in our house. It became a memory wall for me. I had to keep myself busy during this holiday break. To this day, school and sports memorabilia are kept along with Kate and Michael's achievements. Perhaps, not all of our friends understood the concept, but I had to do what I felt was right for me in order to survive, no matter what "others" said.

The anniversaries of Joby's birthday and death were the most difficult milestones that first year. On each of those occasions, we chose to use a demonstrative display to express our grief. For his birthday, we had many of Joby's friends over. All the kids wrote messages to Joby on pieces of paper, and we tied each message to a helium balloon. We then went outside with our balloons, stood in a circle, listened to a song that had lyrics written by his sister Kate, and let our balloons go.

From Kate's song:

I had a brother who was very dear;
I lost him just only last year.
I don't know how I'll ever go on;
I won't see him night or dawn.

He was only sixteen;
Why did God have to be so mean?
He didn't need to take him away;
I won't see him another day.

He is my angel up above;
He is watching over me with his love.
I'll miss him so much,
But I know I'll be fine,
Because he is my angel up above:
He is watching me with his love…

This action was a replication of a special moment the day of Joby's funeral. Teresa Rishel, one of Joby's former teachers, and Karen Abel, a mother of one of Joby's friends, hosted a memorial ceremony after the funeral. They let the teens talk, socialize, have pizza, and remember Joby. Toward the end of the day, a youth minister led them in a prayer and had a helium balloon for each teenager. They made a huge circle in the backyard, said their good-byes to their friend, and let off hundreds of balloons. It must have been a wonderful sight!

May 18, 1998 (from my journal):

*His friends came over, we let off our balloons.
They gathered as friends to remember his friendship.
How Joby would have loved this celebration!
But as quickly as they arrived, it seemed they left with hugs and tears and joy.
Inside I still waited for that miracle.
I waved goodbye to all of them, and I ached for I still couldn't comprehend.*

Writing was another way in which some of us expressed our grief. As I said, my daughter wrote the beautiful lyrical poem about her brother that was later put to music. Our son Michael wrote an essay for school and for a state contest about his brother. He may not have talked openly about Joby, but his thoughts came out in this writing. Michael and Joby were very close brothers and had done practically everything together. Because of this special relationship, I worried about Michael. He wasn't open with his feelings. Yet, I saw Michael working through his grief in his own way. I realized it was necessary not to push him in his journey of grief but rather let him know that I was always there for him. I learned that it was important to let my children know that they could talk about and express their grief without destroying me as the parent.

From Michael's essay:

A big brother, to me, is a gift no one can appreciate until they're gone...It is a love that I miss and will never forget as long as I live. That love that I have for my brother and the memories that I hold close are important to me...

Photos became even more important to us than usual. These were the only ways we could visually remember our child. The same mom who had the balloon launch for Joby's classmates also created, with the help of another mom, a beautiful memory friendship photo album of the day they had their balloon ceremony. This was a wonderful and lasting gift.

My niece Heather later gave us a photo album with various pictures of Joby and writings by family members of what they remembered most about him. Some of them were quite humorous and touching. I am now a true believer that humor had a major role in dealing with grief and healing. I think it was one of the greatest healers for me. I remember the night of Joby's funeral. Dave's family and mine were all together on the back deck of the house. As we overlooked Joby's beautiful garden, we sat around and shared embarrassing moments of our lives. Joby would have loved it. He loved family, and he loved the humor we tend to generate. The laughter was short–lived, but for the moment we laughed, and this time the tears were wept in joy. Humor was a very powerful tool to help us journey through the sorrow.

From my niece's book of Memories of Joby:
(taken from my brother's writing)

...The last time I saw Joby was the first time I visited Rensselaer earlier this year...It was a short but wonderful visit that abounded with laughter, caring, and a genuine love. One of my snapshots from that visit was the ease with which Joby laughed at some of my lame attempts at humor. Even when it wasn't funny, he laughed....
I do know he liked to laugh, and in so doing, lifted the spirits of everyone around him.

    I also had our last family photo copied for my children and extended family members. I framed the photos for my children and put them in their bedrooms. In this way, I tried not to hide the pain of losing Joby but rather celebrate the existence of his short life.
    During visits from Joby's friends this first year, I also made the decision to give away several of his possessions. This was a logical decision for me because I felt Joby would want his friends to have them. I know for some parents this is not a step to be taken quickly. I felt that my son could live vicariously through his things with his friends. I think giving them some of his personal items (tee shirts, hats, keepsakes) helped his dear friends come to grips with losing a friend like Joby. I still have a box of the rest of my son's clothes, baseball cards, and other mementos. I am not rushing myself to part with them; in time, I am sure I will know what to do with them.

August 30, 1997 (from my journal):

As you know, Joby, I've been giving things of yours to your friends. I want you to live on somehow in all of us.

Some of the "action" steps of grief are more subtle than the ones I have mentioned. When the death of a child who is still living at home occurs, the decision about what to do with their bedroom becomes monumental. For me, the decision was made through necessity. Five months after Joby's death, I noticed Kate sleeping in his bedroom. Joby's room was across the hall from his brother Mike's, and Kate was in a downstairs bedroom across from ours. I noticed this nightly routine of hers. She would go up at night to sleep and then come back downstairs in the morning to get ready for school. I finally approached her about moving her bedroom upstairs. This was not an easy decision. So many parents I had spoken with hadn't even touched their son's or daughter's bedroom in years.

I think Kate felt not only closer to Joby up in his room but also closer to Michael. It took some time for Michael to adjust to this change; but once he did, he and his sister developed an even closer relationship. Whether or not I should have touched Joby's room was no longer an issue; I felt I had to make the change, and I did. Things were getting "different" and this was one of those needed changes in order to continue our grieving process.

As I look back, I probably did more that first year in physical demonstration of my grief because it allowed me to expend energy and thought in a positive way. Even returning to work helped me fill many empty voids. It gave me direction that I so desperately needed that first year. All these "actions" became extensions of our grief. They became ways for all of us to tap into the process and go forward in the journey. The physical steps allowed us to feel not so helpless.

I believe all of these actual physical actions helped channel the mixed emotions that we were all experiencing. Whether they were actions by us, family, or friends of Joby's, we all discovered that the physical displays of memorials became important. They helped us direct the grief into positive directions.

I think this Step Three of "Taking Action" was a pivotal one for us that first year. It was the most therapeutic step to help my family and me endure those dreaded "firsts" of everything that first year brings.

Thoughts during that first year
(from my journal):

Not a day goes by that I don't ache.
Each night is a reminder that I will awaken without you.
I feel as if I am just existing, not living.
My work has little meaning now—
I struggle to see the joys that life once brought to us.
I can so vividly remember nights lying in bed and thanking God for my wonderful life and my wonderful children.
But now, my breath is taken from me;
It is a perpetual ache.
We will never be the same.

You, son, were a link between us all for you touched so many.
How could we have been so lucky to have you?
And now be so unlucky to lose you?

The Second Year After His Death

The Second Year After His Death

Making it through that first year was monumental, but the journey of grief continued. I think the second year was even more of a mixed emotional bag than the first. After the first year of that "frozen in time" feeling and numbness, the sensations of pain became more real. The emotional fog was lifting from the first year, the loss of our child was now becoming a stark reality. No matter how many times Joby's friends would visit, or how many times I would work on something in his memory, none of these things brought my son back. There were so many times that I wished I could go back to bed, and the nightmare would be over.

Perhaps I was in denial when I created all those memorials during the first year. Maybe in the back of my mind, I thought they were ways I could bring Joby back to life, but this year was a harsh reminder that those memorials would not perform miracles. My son was gone. How was I to accept this? I wanted him back! I believe this second year marked a growing "anger stage" that I had read about in so many grief books.

❑ ❑ ❑ ❑

STEP ONE: Taking Care of You and Yours:

I made some important observations—the first of which was that each of us in the immediate family grieved differently than we did in the first year. This was one of the most difficult changes to accept. I noticed my husband's demonstration of grief changing. I remained more open about it; he kept more to himself. I didn't realize at the time that the loss of Joby was just too painful for him to talk about anymore, and he was doing what he had to do in his journey. Instead of accepting this change, I resented it, and my husband resented me talking about Joby or sharing pictures with him.

We were embarking on our own individual journeys of grief and didn't realize the conflicts that were developing. I was devouring grief book after grief book and naturally thought my husband would want to share in the reading. Because it was so helpful for me, I thought reading would also help him. He didn't want to read about someone else's pain; he was trying to forget his own. Both of us were living moment to moment in our own little world. I thought we were doing "so well" that first year, and now in this second year we were barely connecting with each other.

I once read that 75% of marriages end in a divorce after the death of a child. Dave and I had already been through a lot in our marriage. I knew Joby would want us to work this out together and not have his loss tear the family apart. It was then that I made a commitment to work it out. I sought out a grief counselor.

***From a poem my husband wrote about
our son during this second year:***

*Other Angels must be sad,
not to have the life you had!
Your life was short, but your*

*love was strong.
Sometimes it's a blessing not
to live too long.
...Your sins were so few, your
smile was so great
God had to be "beaming"
as you entered His gate.*

*Other Angels must be sad
not to have the life you had.
But sadder than all the
Angels that fly
is the sadness felt
by your mother and "I".
We miss you still, to
the Heaven's we cry.
We'll miss you Joby, till the
day that we die!*

I also found myself reaching out to my children more since I felt distanced from my husband, but this was too heavy a burden for them. With changes in their lives, they were trying to adjust the best they could. I felt as if I was the odd peg in this family wheel, trying to keep it together yet not quite fitting in.

For Dave and me, the counseling was a slow process. We found a counselor through friends and went to see her once a week. This was an out–of–town drive and since both of us worked, we had to adjust our schedules and agree that these sessions took priority over any other commitments.

I should have recognized that Dave and I had not

really been grieving in the same way from the start. Although we were there for each other on demand that first year, I hadn't noticed we were grieving differently until that second year. This shouldn't be surprising since men and women tend to solve problems differently, prioritize things differently, express their love differently. Why couldn't men and women experience grief differently? The sooner I accepted this difference, the better I handled my own grief.

The counseling continued through the second year, and my husband and I were encouraged to make that night after counseling "date night." So, we did. We went out to dinner after our sessions. No matter what our schedules were, those Wednesdays were counseling/date night for us. After some of our sessions, I really didn't feel like trying to bond with Dave, and I'm sure there were times he didn't feel like trying to bond with me. We forced ourselves to work through some of our frustrations during the meal. Some nights the discussions were tense, and I am surprised we even got home together. Yet, there were those sparks of hope and understanding because we were the only ones who really knew what each was going through.

What we did with those Wednesdays was what I was trying to do every day of the week. I discovered that Dave was far more receptive to this one–day–a–week sharing than the daily sharing we had been doing the first year. This was a major step in the transition of the journey of grief. "Date night" became our weekly ritual. As the second year progressed, it was an anticipated time not only for Dave and me but also for our children. This time away from Kate and Michael gave them private time with each other. A parent can't possibly fulfill every need of a child, any more than a spouse can possibly fulfill every need of a mate.

I also believed our "date nights" showed our children that adults need to work together to get through life's major crises. The nights away from the house gave Michael and Kate time to talk about their day, to talk about how crazy we were becoming, and to spend time together without us around. I believe this has helped them develop the very special bond that they still have today.

Another observation I made was the difference between a sister's grief and a brother's grief. With my son Michael, the anger of losing his brother began to affect his actions at school. He was never a bad student, but I noticed that he was very defensive about his brother and in things in general. Like his dad, he kept the emotion to himself, and the grief would spill out in other ways.

I began to see signs of distress in some of his behavior in wrestling. He was on the varsity wrestling team as a sophomore, and I think he felt more intensity in this sport because the last time his brother Joby wrestled was as a sophomore. Mike's wrestling was far more emotional than it had been. I could tell he often wrestled for his brother or in memory of his brother. This was something that was tearing him apart, and he would eventually change this motivation.

In fact, during that wrestling season, we all learned that none of us were immune to more tragedy. It was only five months before Joby died that my mother had passed away. Then during this second year after his death, my father–in–law passed away. Dave, Kate, and I had flown down to Florida for his funeral. Michael remained back home with friends of ours so he could win his sophomore wrestling tournament in memory of his "Grandpa Mike." The morning we were to return home, we got a phone call. Dave got the message that "Michael had been in a car accident, and it didn't look good." At that moment, I remembered a mother I met from Compassionate Friends who had told me she lost two sons within two years. I kept thinking that this just can't be happening again! The flight home was endless. I had to keep reminding myself that no fear was greater than what we had already faced.

After arriving at the Indianapolis Airport, we somehow made our way back to Rensselaer in record time and went directly to our local hospital. We were told that Michael had been driving back to our farm early that winter morning before going to wrestling practice at school so he could feed the horses. His Tracker had slipped on a patch of black ice, and he lost control of the sliding vehicle. His car rolled over three times before it landed upside down, resting on its crushed hood between two trees. A farmer behind him witnessed the entire accident. When he got to our son's car, Michael was hanging upside down but still strapped in by his seat belt. Michael was unconscious and the farmer feared he was dead. We were so very lucky this time to find our son alive. He was cut and bruised, but alive!

Obviously, Michael's wrestling season was ended for that year, and that was another disappointment for him. However, members of his wrestling team still supported him. In fact, that first night of the accident, they were all crowded around his bed and when I entered Michael's hospital room, I could see the look of fear, yet hope, on my son's face. Michael's accident was another harsh reminder that life doesn't stop for any of us and death is always only a breath away. It made us realize that the journey continues for all of us and perhaps we are all on borrowed time. Therefore, appreciating every moment we have with our loved ones is a very sacred thing.

Kate was entering seventh grade. She was far more open with her grief than her brother. In fact, she became a comfort for me during a lot of emotional times. She often told me of her fear that she had not been a "good sister" for Joby because it was sometimes difficult for her to remember his voice. Reassuring her that this was a normal feeling and part of the grieving process was a major part of our talks. She and I did more sharing of our feelings than did the men in of the family during that second year. We were lucky to have one another.

I realized I needed to think of different ways to help both of my children deal with their sorrow. During that second year, I made a point to go up to their bedrooms every night. No matter how the day went, I would always go up and check on them. Those late night visits with the kids became very valuable for us. That is not to say that there were not times that we were all quick to anger.

Just the tiniest of things could set us off. Back then I didn't realize that even Kate had thought she was doing something to upset me. It wasn't until two more years into this journey that she would admit this to me. I have felt so bad that I caused her such unnecessary stress, but she now better understands how grief can affect each of us.

I mention this now to alert the reader that this may happen in your own situation. It would be helpful to keep this in mind and try to discuss these multitude shifts of feelings and emotions with your children. Also, keep in mind, that as you progress through this journey, you will regain an understanding of your own emotions and actions.

Not only as their mom, but as a teacher, I was concerned about how Kate and Michael's grief would affect their grades and work in school. This was something I could not ignore. I believe it was important that they didn't use grief as an excuse for poor behavior or poor grades. They didn't. I felt fortunate that they did well in school considering all they had been experiencing.

From Michael's essay about his brother:

If God needed an angel, He got the best one I can think of. Having him for 16 years is better than not having him here at all. Joby is worth a thousand memories that will stay locked in my heart forever. I embrace them all.

I really began to struggle with teaching. I was entering my nineteenth year of teaching and, though I used to enjoy teaching, my life had changed. I must admit that going back to work helped me deal with daily pain of grief, but my emotions at work now were drained more quickly than before. I worked at a different high school than where my children attended, and it became difficult to work with some of the more apathetic 16-year-olds in class. Teaching apathetic students certainly was nothing new for an experienced high school teacher, but I began to compare them with my son Joby. I would become impatient and angered when I saw how they were wasting their lives and yet my son didn't have a chance to make more out of his! This attitude was unfair to my students as well as to me.

I was determined that I would have to make some drastic changes in my own career. The next year I would be turning 50; it was the start of the new millennium; and it would be a chance for me to symbolically make changes in my life. It was during this second year after Joby's death that I started entertaining the idea of retiring from teaching. I have always worked since college, so a decision to "retire early" was not an easy choice.

Physically, I noticed personal changes. I seemed to be losing stamina. I noticed that my hair was falling out. I would be in the shower shampooing my hair and notice clumps of my hair in my hand. There were mornings the water washed over many of my tears and handfuls of my hair. I knew I had to find more positive channels for this grief. I had to listen to my body more closely and not push myself.

My priorities, needs, and wants were all getting redefined. This was also happening to my husband and to my children. They were changing and redefining their own lives. It was imperative that we tried to be kinder and more patient with one another. Realizing this was hard because I was now feeling anger and confusion, but as I have mentioned earlier, it is so important to keep the lines of communication open between family members.

Unfortunately, I began to relive the nightmare of the accident. It seemed every time I closed my eyes, I saw my dead son lying on that emergency table. I tried not to think about every detail but it haunted me. Some days seemed to pass at such a slow pace that I had to consciously do something to take my mind off the pain. My sister Holly gave me good advice when she told me, "Brenda, when your head gets thinking about only one thing, it's time to do something else." This was great advice not only then but for the years to come.

☐ ☐ ☐ ☐

STEP TWO: Relating to Others:

During the second year, I heard from others, "You really need to be getting over this…" even more. I had to remind myself that these people didn't know what they were talking about and didn't say these things maliciously. My husband and I made a point to continue sharing with other grieving parents to discuss where we were in the grief process. We found these meetings very comforting. I also found myself more empathic to mothers who had recently lost a child and would send comforting notes to them as so many other mothers did for me the first year. I also sent these mothers many of the grief books that I had read to these mothers. Perhaps I was still trying to make sense of my own loss by helping others.

The second year seemed to be even more challenging to be participate happily in family gatherings or parties with friends. I found it increasingly difficult to enjoy myself around groups of people. I began to decline offers to social gatherings that I had grudgingly accepted in last year. I can recall a time or two when I even lashed out at my own sisters and asked them not to bother me anymore. I often found it difficult to talk to them over the phone. The effort to chat about my day was inconceivable to me. At that time, I felt the family members were intrusive and made it difficult for me to silently grieve. Though, I knew they were only checking up on me out of concern.

I am grateful that my sisters were forgiving. They allowed me the space and time I needed to get through this "anger" stage.

I know a lot of our friends had difficulty in understanding why I never wanted to go out or have a group of people over since my husband would make suggestions that we do so. I think since I was teaching all day, I was more emotionally drained than usual. When I came home, my emotions came pouring out. This was a very exhausting process for me as well as for my family, so going out with friends or family was the last thing I wanted to do.

June 7, 1998 (from my journal):

There are times like today I find solace in being by myself.
It's almost as if I seek refuge in being alone.
The pain of losing Joby is often too great for me to bear. Why don't others understand?
How can they possibly think I am having fun in this materialistic world?

As with any fatal accident, there was an investigatory process involving the police and various insurance companies. In dealing with both issues, it became a most difficult time for my family because we had to relive the day of the accident all over again. Time varies for each individual situation, but for us this took months and seemed to drag on unnecessarily. It was during the second year after the accident when all of these legal proceedings were finally finished. I remember it clearly because it was like an albatross had been lifted from us. At that moment, we felt hope in regaining our lives, but it was still a slow process.

As the holidays approached, I experienced anxiety attacks around groups of people. I still didn't want to be with anyone. Nevertheless, we went to Kentucky for Thanksgiving as we always did and somehow we made it through another holiday without Joby. To be honest, I don't remember a thing about that Thanksgiving except that I missed my son just as much as I did the first year. When Christmas drew near, my anxiety increased, and I made a decision to do something that I thought I would never do.

During the first year after my son's death, I had been reading a myriad of books on grief and spirituality. I decided to contact someone for a "spiritual" reading. I located a recommended psychic intuitive Char Margolis and made a spontaneous call to her on December 16th. I reached her answering service and learned that she was in Hollywood making a television show. The woman I talked with, however, sensed my urgency and said that if I wanted to talk to Char, maybe she could make some time for me soon over the phone. I agreed; but after hanging up, I thought, "What am I doing? This is nuts!"

Two days later on December 18, I received a call saying that I would be able to talk with this renowned psychic in an hour. There was no obligation but if I wanted to speak with her, I needed to call her at that time. I hung up the phone and confided with my family.

Of course, they all thought I had gone off the deep end, and I realized I was getting no support from them. It was up to me. After an hour's wait, I made the decision and went into my bedroom, shut the door, and made the call.

The next hour was indescribable. Without getting into too much detail, all I can say is that Char began telling me things about my son's burial that only my immediate family knew. From the start, I never mentioned to her who died in my family or why I was calling or gave her any names. The fact that I had lost loved ones (my son, mother, father, and brother) was never discussed before the reading. It was uncanny the things that she knew.

She started the reading by citing the death of my mother. She said that her name was "Adeline or something like that" (her name was Adelaide) "but she wanted to be called Addy" (which was true), and that "Addy met John" (John Robert is Joby's given name). She rattled off my dad's name "Raymond" and then stumbled with my brother's fairly unusual name "Roderick." She began to tell me how "all of them met John." She said that "John knew Michael was having trouble in dealing with all of this but let him know that he (John) was okay."

Char went on to say that John wanted "Kathy… or…Kate to know that he comes to her in her dreams." She told me how we cremated John (later in the reading, she referred to him as "Jobe") in his "special hat and sports outfit." (We had cremated Joby in his favorite Oakley hat and his golf outfit.) She also told me that we buried a "special photo with him" (which we did).

She also said that "Jobe loved all the flowers" (which I took as his garden) and "he loved the fact that so many were wearing his shirts." I was taking notes on all that was transpiring over the phone, but tears began to streak down my face in amazement over the accuracy of the many details. My only regret is that I didn't tape the conversation over the phone, but I really had not spent any time in preparation for this.

She concluded the reading by saying that "Jobe had work to do on the other side" and that "he wanted me to know that his dog was with him." This may have been one of the most amazing parts for me. I said that that couldn't be because his dog Boomer was with us. "No," she said, "it was a Benji–looking dog that was jumping on him." She said he was saying something about "Raz or something like that." I about dropped the phone! When Joby was a little boy, we lived in North Carolina, and I had a shaggy little dog named "Rags." I had to have this dog put to sleep right before my family and I moved back to Indiana. Joby had always known that Rags was my dog even before I was married, and that she had always been my favorite pet. Very few people here in Rensselaer, where we have lived for the past 11 years, even knew of this dog. So, it was such a shock for this woman to bring this up from my past!

I could only sit there on the floor and scramble to get down everything that was said. Before, we hung up, she asked me exactly how he died and how old he was, and I told her. Then a weird connection was made. I was talking with her on December 18 and possibly communicating with my son; his birthday is on March 18, and he was killed on May 18. Of course, she told me that was no coincidence; I have to wonder. I hung up the phone and quickly went into the other room where my husband was watching television. "Well?" he asked.

I sat down beside him and told him, "I'm just not

sure. Listen," and I began to read back my notes to him. I read and he sat in silence. I looked up after I finished reading, and tears were streaming down his face.

He softly replied, "And just what are you not sure about?" He said we had to get our children together and read this to them. I did.

I shared these notes with my family at Christmas. I could tell there were some family members who remained skeptical and thought that I possibly "made–up" this information for my own peace of mind. Yet, I could also tell that some were touched by the details, especially with the accuracy about our parents and older brother. I shared my notes with many other people; and each time I shared them, I became certain that we can't possibly know all there is to know about death and a possible after–life. This carried me through Step Two of "Relating to Others."

☐ ☐ ☐ ☐

STEP THREE: Taking Action:

Physically, I dove into caring for and expanding my son's garden. It had now survived all four seasons of the year, and it grew in shape as it meandered across the back yard. I added Shasta daisies, more irises, violet and yellow day lilies, white and yellow daffodils, cone flowers, thyme, tall grasses, and more. Memorabilia of angel and animal statues, a sun dial, and sentimental rocks (with inspirational messages engraved upon them) were added to his grave site. I hung angel and butterfly wind chimes from three of the four Hawthorn trees that anchored the garden. It flourished as did my love for him. I spent hours weeding and working in the garden until the winter months approached. Like the first year, I found this "action" step to be extremely helpful.

During that second fall, I made another decision to give back to the school that helped us out so much during that first year. I was maintaining Joby's scholarship, but I had a new idea. I inquired if the school would like an Academic Hall of Excellence where they could honor top academic students; they were quite receptive.

It took the rest of this second year for the hallway to come to fruition but it was worth the wait. I had one of Joby's classmates sketch Joby's face from a photograph, and then had this drawing etched onto a plaque with these words:

*This Academic Hall of Excellence
is dedicated to the
CLASS of 1999
and
JOBY GREENE
(March 18, 1981–May 18, 1997)
A fellow classmate, teammate, and friend*

I wanted to recognize his classmates for all they had done for our family and for keeping his memory alive in so many ways. A framed group picture of the top 15% of his graduating class was the first group of students to be displayed in the Academic Hall.

My husband and I purchased enough matching frames to last for the next twenty years and contracted a friend to mount the frames on the wall. We also had a beautiful Amish handmade oak sign, proclaiming "Academic Hall of Excellence," and it was hung above all the frames alongside the memorial plaque.

During that same fall, I took another action that I thought I would never do again. I got a fourth dog! First before I share this story, I must explain that shortly before Joby was killed, I took the boys up to a mastiff breeder just north of town to see the dogs. When we got home, Joby told me that he wanted a fawn colored male pup and would call it Mr. Bojangles. When Joby died, the breeder wanted to give us a pup but we ended up purchasing Maggie, our apricot mastiff pup Christmas of '97, because she was the only pup of that first litter. When the second litter arrived, the following happened as I wrote in my journal:

September 7, 1998 (from my journal):

I must record another strange event before I forget. The mastiff breeder called me last week. She informed me that a couple from Chicago had returned a pup from her second litter. Did I want it? She reminded me that she had promised to give me a pup (after Joby died) if it were a fawn colored male and this pup was just that. Out of curiosity, Michael and I went to see the puppy. Yes, it was a five month old, fawn colored male. I asked if the previous owners had named it. "Yes," replied her husband, " I believe Bo was a nickname."

"Short for Beauregard?" I asked.

"No, that wasn't the name," he said.

I looked over at Michael, then back at the

The Second Year

> breeder's husband and slowly asked, "Not, Bojangles?"
> "Yes, that's it!"
> That is when the decision was made for us.
> Joby now had his Mr. Bojangles.

In that same journal entry, I had also recorded another irony that I think is worthy of noting. I was realizing even more that some things in life just could not be explained. I wrote:

> Dave is gone fishing in Wyoming, rained last night and I couldn't sleep.
> Tried to think of Joby and then suddenly the bedroom door flew open.
> I took Maggie and went outside to inspect—nothing was found.
> I felt Joby's presence and just prayed for one more time to talk to him, to see his face, to hear him laugh, I miss everything about him.

During Christmas of '98, there would be another "first" that would become a tradition for my family. I had been given a suggestion by a friend about a prayer reading that was a beautiful way to remember our loved ones. This person told me about a prayer that is used with four candles and that each candle would represent one of the following: Sadness, Memories, Determination, and Love. As the candles are being lit, the following prayer is to be read:

From My Son's Garden

As we light these four candles in your honor, we light one for our sadness, one for our memories, one for our determination, and one for our love.

We light this candle for our sadness. The pain of losing you is intense, and the grief we feel is often hard to handle. We want you to know that we miss you so much.

We light this candle for our memories. There is so much we remember—your smile, your laugh—the good times and the bad one, too—when we were happy—all those times that never could have been lived with anyone but you. We want you to know that we will always remember.

We light this candle for our determination. Knowing you has brought us strength. We are changed because of you. Your life has made a difference in our lives. We want you to know that we will take the energy of your living to help us move forward in our lives.

We light this candle for our love. The specialness that we shared with you can never be replaced. During this holiday season, our love for you will shine as brightly as this candle. We will pass that love on to others, and as we do, our hearts will smile because of you. We want you to know that we will always love you.

I had mentioned this idea only to my sister Carol, who hosts our family Christmas, and told her that I would like someone to read this and light four candles. She loved the idea, and she and I were going to present this to the rest of the family on Christmas Day. Ironically, when my family and I arrived at my sister's for Christmas, we found that my brother (who knew nothing about the prayer) had made a candle holder for four candles. On his wooden candle holder, he had painted the following words:

Love is forever,
Memories are forever.
Those we love
are never really lost.

This inscription had been on a card that I sent to him just days before Joby was killed. My brother not only made the candle holder with the above words inscribed on it but he also had them engraved on a rock that I have at Joby's grave site. It has now become a tradition in our house to say this prayer and light the four candles. We do this as we stand in a circle holding hands. It has become a wonderful way to openly express our love and remember those who are physically not with us. It was a major step for my immediate family and me.

As for the very emotional anniversaries of Joby's birth and death, we continued with some of the physical actions we did the first year. We continued the balloon tradition on the second anniversary of Joby's birthday, and the anniversary of his death came and quietly left with our prayers and the lighting of a candle. These milestone events were conducted just with the immediate family this second year. There were quiet and difficult times for us. I think, Dave, Mike, Kate and I were beginning to realize that these dates were no different than any other day without Joby. We missed him everyday.

Before I knew it, May was approaching and it was a time for Joby's classmates to graduate. How could I face this? Do I attend his "would–be" graduation? Do I go to any graduation parties when I really should be planning my own? Joby's class had already given us a large senior photo (signed by his classmates), a senior mug with all of the seniors' names (including Joby's), a senior T–shirt, and senior graduating tassels to which they had added green strands in his memory. So, I was already feeling a part of this graduation year.

The entire month of May was an emotional battle for me. I had made the decision to be very active in this graduation, but my husband took just the opposite approach. He felt participating in all of these events would be too painful. I, on the other hand, was dealing with my grief differently so I decided to become involved. I first decided to speak at the Seniors' Baccalaureate.

I clearly remember the day I was working on my presentation. One night about a month before Baccalaureate, I was trying to come up with a song that I wanted sung in dedication to his class. I was in my husband's old pick–up truck with my daughter Kate, and I was driving her home from swimming practice. I asked her, "What song do you think I should use?" Immediately, the truck died as another car was approaching! I coasted off to the side and the approaching car passed by us. A bit rattled, I remarked how I hated that truck. I started it up again, and the song "Angel" by Sara McLachlan began to play on the radio. I just smiled and said, "Well, I guess that's the song!"

I asked a friend of mine Ned Tonner (an attorney in town and one of my former students) to sing the song. He graciously agreed. When Baccalaureate rolled around, Dave, Michael, and Kate joined me in attendance. I gave my speech, had the song sung, and my family and I joined the students after the ceremonies. Everyone began to mingle. I watched Dave as he walked over to Joby's best friend (who was in the accident), put his arms around him and whispered, "I forgive you." It was an emotional night for all of us. I believe it was one of the first steps toward healing for my husband.

During the next week, I received many letters from Joby's friends; and I, too, was sending them letters and buying them graduation gifts. However, I still had Senior Awards Night to get through and then graduation. Shortly before awards night is when Dave told me he was going on a fishing trip with his uncle, and he was planning to take our son Michael.

I reminded him his trip was right in the middle of Senior Awards Night and Graduation. I was furious. Dave had responded, "Look, Joby isn't graduating. Why should we put ourselves through this!" I couldn't understand his point-of-view then, but I do now. I must admit that later he did offer to change his plans; however, I had already contacted Cheryl and Carol, my sisters, to be with me during the night of awards and graduation. I reluctantly told him to go on the trip with Michael. I realize now that he did what was right for him, just as I had to do what I felt was right for me.

That year we gave four $1200 scholarships. I knew we would be really dipping into the funds. As with most scholarships, Joby's is funded by private donations. However, I knew Joby would want me to help as many of his classmates as I could so this would be the only year that we could offer this amount. Senior Awards Night was a long and emotional one. However, with the help of my sisters and my daughter Kate, I got through it!

From a poem written by Staci Hamstra (a good friend of Joby's):

I have a very special friend
With whom I share my love
Although he is not here with me,
He's watching from above.

It's been a year since he's been gone
And not a day goes by
That I don't stop and think of him
And tears come to my eye.

...The reason why God took his life
I do not understand
He was so young, just 16 years
I know it was God's plan.

Although it just does not seem fair
It was his time to die
I'm looking forward to the day
I'll join him in the sky.

Graduation was the next day. We all scurried around getting ready, and I thought I was ready to face the graduation that my son John Robert Greene would never be able to attend. I wore my green ribbon proudly. My sisters, my daughter, and I got out of the car and walked into the already crowded gymnasium. It was hot and stuffy and I felt as if everyone was looking at me.

Then the processional began. Here they came. Many students entered with their green ribbons displayed on their gowns, the green and red and black graduation tassels hanging from their hats. I spotted all of Joby's dear friends. As I glanced at the graduation seats, I spotted the row of G's. Next to Kelly Gudeman would have been John Robert Greene but on his chair his classmates had laid his graduation gown and hat in his memory. My heart soared; they didn't forget him even after two years! How I loved those young adults; I was proud of their sensitivity and their outward display of caring!

By now, tears began to stream down my face. I think only then did I really come to see for myself that Joby would not be forgotten. How could I have doubted any of them? One of my sisters leaned over to me and whispered, "Do you want to leave, Brenda?" I sat there, frozen in grief and pride all at the same time. I nodded yes. As quickly and silently as we had entered that crowded gymnasium, we made our way out. At that point, Cheryl and Carol decided to get Kate and me out of town and drive to our sister Holly's farm in Ohio. There was no need to attend any graduation parties, and I knew they would all understand.

During that summer after graduation, editorials appeared by Joby's friends and myself sharing our thoughts about the closeness of this class. The unique relationship this group of young teens had for each other as a result of

Joby's death was apparent. Yes, perhaps I was seeing some "good" coming forth from my most devastating loss.

Like the first year, I found the "action" steps of all the physical displays of our grief the most helpful, but I must admit I knew I was facing a major personal change. Throughout the second year, I was skating on emotional thin ice. At work, I continued to struggle in concentrating and making it through each day. By the time I got home, finished meal time, finished my homework, tried to help the kids with their work, and attended one of our children's sports events, I was absolutely drained physically and emotionally. I was certain now that something would have to change.

May 5, 1999 (from my journal):

I want life different; I want to be free from all of this.
Grief is such an exhausting process, one wants to avoid it but if you do, You just must face it even harder at the next turn.
I have come to that crossroads, Stepping back, I think, Facing it...working through it...is a good thing.

The Third Year After His Death

The Third Year After His Death

The third year was more difficult to recollect than the first and second, yet I made major changes in my own life. It was a year of slow acceptance of our son's death, and we were constantly reminded that grief was a continual process. I believe it was at this point I knew I would be dealing with this grief every day of my life. Therefore, I had to come to grips with that. I discovered there were other stages in this journey of grief, and I couldn't let myself get stuck in just one. This realization helped me to grow emotionally and to slowly begin to heal.

March 22, 1999 (from my journal):

Sliding in and out of pain and loss.
One can't possibly understand the inner wretchedness that occurs to lose a child so abruptly, a child with whom our souls touched.

☐ ☐ ☐ ☐

STEP ONE: Taking Care of You and Yours:

I did things for me that I thought I couldn't do! I had struggled with my own purpose in life for two years, and I had struggled with my personal relationships. I knew I was desperately in need of a change. My job at school was creating more problems for me than I could handle, so I tried changing things at work. I tried to do new projects at school by working on new elective courses and writing new curriculums for my classes. These changes, however, were not effective in helping me develop a new direction in my life. The stress and responsibilities from school were now tearing me apart. Was I weaker than I once was? No, I was different. In order to pursue my journey of grief, I had to change course. I knew that my current teaching career was coming to an end.

Dave and I continued with our counseling and weekly date nights. We were gradually making progress. There were times when the prospect of us staying together just didn't look good; however, there was a new bond forming between us. We couldn't hold on to what we once had because what we were facing and living through now was different. Our relationship had to change; otherwise, grief would destroy our union.

March 25, 1999 (from my journal):

We drift further apart, like floating out to sea.
He in his world as if trapped by choice.
I in mine and tired of trying to connect.
Though he sits right there, he seems millions
of miles away from me. We must think of ways
of coming together...I need this footing...

Changing our relationship was not an easy thing to do. Through this year of counseling, we learned that more than ever we both needed to listen more carefully to one another. We needed to stay on the main issues that really were troubling us. Sometimes, it was easy for us to attack everything that was bothering us and blame it on each other. We learned the importance of dealing with one issue at a time just in the same way we had to still deal with our grief: one day at a time. I believe the commitment not to let this loss destroy us kept us together.

Kate and Michael seemed to have a better grip on their grief than they did before. They seemed far more resilient in getting back to their daily lives than Dave or me. By the third year, the need to live for their brother's memory, I don't believe, was as strong as it was during that second year. Michael was a junior now, and this had a major impact on him because he was now at an age that his older brother never reached. This was also a change for us as parents because we no longer could refer back to what Joby had done at the same age. Michael's junior year was a learning experience for all of us.

He struggled from time to time; I could tell. One of the struggles he had was dealing with the Greene Room and the possibility that it was going to be dissolved. He had immediately joined the Greene Room when he was a sophomore. In spite of all of his attempts to keep the "club" going in a positive memory of his brother, the personality of the group was beginning to change. He had to deal with negative behavior by some of the new members who hadn't been friends of Joby's. This was totally unacceptable for Michael, and he knew that the dissolution of the group was imminent. The group dissolved the third year after his brother's death. I don't know for sure, but maybe this was a weight off Mike. We were all discovering changes in our lives, and these were inevitable in order to survive.

Kate, on the other hand, was finishing up her years at the middle school. She was in the eighth grade and, like most eighth graders, she was ready to move on to high school. She continued to be there emotionally for me. I felt our bond was getting stronger. I think she also was creating a stronger bond with Michael. She admired her big brother and enjoyed being with him. He promised her when she entered high school, he would help her out and be there for her.

March 3, 1999 (from my journal):

I have struggled with Michael and Kate but my love for them is unconditional. I will always be there for them and we shall ride these waves together.

September 11, 1999 (from my journal):

I have grown closer to Michael and Kate. I feel Michael is now there for me...he is developing a closeness to me that I treasure. Kate has always been there for me...she is my steadfast joy.

It seemed this third year, we still were learning the differences in which each of was dealing with our own grief. However, we continued to place the help from one another as top priority. I can't emphasize enough the importance of keeping the lines of communication open within your immediate family. Even though Kate and Michael seemed to find solace with friends more than us, there were times that they struggled. It was at this time, that many of their friends were not as demonstrative as they were before with their understanding and had to be reminded that Kate and Michael were still dealing with their brother's death. It is important to note this as a parent because just as some of your friends and family may not relate to your own continual pain, you must keep in mind that your own children are probably experiencing the same distance from some of their friends. That is why it is essential to help each other realize that none of us are alone in experiencing this stage of grief.

▫ ▫ ▫ ▫

STEP TWO: Relating to Others:

The third year after Joby's death, I saw many changes in my immediate family as well as in relationships with other people in our lives. I still wasn't ready to jump full force into parties and family holidays. It was during this year that I made decisions to do things that I knew in my heart I had to do for my own emotional well-being. I would graciously decline invitations and not push myself going on family trips when I really didn't want to. However, I must admit by the end of the third year, this too would change.

When the third Thanksgiving festivities rolled around for our family, I still felt I was living a charade. I dreaded the thought of trying to be thankful and excited to see everyone because all I could think about was that my son wasn't here. This year there would be a major change.

Dave, Mike, Kate, and I would always have to leave Dave's family in Kentucky early so we could make it to the boys' annual wrestling tournament back in northern Indiana. However, this Thanksgiving was to be in Atlanta, Georgia, making it too far for all of us to do both. I saw this as an opportunity to avoid a major family gathering. So, I quickly volunteered to stay home with Michael and watch him wrestle at the two day tournament while Dave took Kate to Georgia to be with the rest of the family. I wasn't trying to be rude; I just felt too emotionally drained to face another big get-together with so many people. This would be the very first holiday that our family was separated.

This separation turned out not to be the best choice after all. What was good for me wasn't good for my immediate family. All four of us disliked the fact that we were separated during such a special time. After this Thanksgiving we vowed never to be separated again for the holidays.

Christmas came and we once again joined my family at my sister's house in Danville, Indiana. I was hoping that I could find the Christmas cheer of the past, but it was still difficult to be with everyone. I believe family members tried to make a conscious effort to make the holidays easier on us, but Dave and I still had difficulty enjoying them. I continued to act strong but it was frustrating for me because there was always that constant empty feeling that my family was not entirely together.

I observed that others would rarely bring up my son's name in conversations, and I would make a point to talk about him. I tried to gently remind my friends and family that not mentioning Joby was the worst thing they could do to me. I wanted to make sure that my child would not be lost in our conversations.

Yet, I tried consciously not to dwell on the loss either. If all I could do was talk about Joby, I was making others feel uncomfortable yet I needed to talk about him. The paradox of dealing with this tragedy was constant.

I continued my relationships with some of the parents Dave and I had met that first year through Compassionate Friends. Dave, on the other hand, didn't feel a need to do so. We continued to have different needs in our grief process and even in our relationship with other people.

As for me, I realized that it was time to make a major transition in my career. I gave notice of my decision to retire from teaching shortly after the holidays. During that last semester of school, I felt relieved. I was glad I had finally acted on my decision to retire. I think Kate and Michael were truly happy for me and felt I deserved a break. I couldn't have asked for more support from my husband. I knew this was a major decision for all of us because my retirement affected all of us. I felt guilty about not bringing home financial support for my family because I have worked outside the home most of my adult life.

I wanted so desperately to discover a new purpose for living and to finally be at home for Kate and Michael. But, most of all, I felt relieved in the fact that I could now face my grief alone and work through it during the day. Weighing the consequences, I knew in my heart that this was the right decision at that time for all of us.

Toward the end of the third year, a major event occurred that made me realize that I was growing in my journey of grief. Joby's favorite cousin (my brother's son

Ryan) got married in Virginia. In fact, the wedding was a month before the third anniversary of Joby's death. I can honestly say that was the very first big family get-together that I actually looked forward to attending since my son's death. Ryan and his new wife Beth celebrated a moment in Joby's honor by playing "American Pie" (ironically, one of Joby's and Ryan's favorite songs) at the wedding reception.

It was a glorious feeling, and instead of gasping for breath in pain like my earlier grief would cause me to do, I smiled with tears and thoroughly enjoyed the moment. Why? Because I felt Joby was there enjoying this honor with us. This was a monumental step for me because it had taken exactly three years since my son's death for me to actually enjoy the company of others. My relationship with others and my ability to share in other people's joy had changed dramatically from how I was during the holidays just five months earlier.

June 18, 2000 (from my journal):

I want to find a purpose of my life as well as a purpose for my son's death. Are they intertwined? I am trying to find some sort of control in my life...
I must take my own direction. I must do this for myself, and no one can do this for me.

☐ ☐ ☐ ☐

STEP THREE: Taking Action:

The action steps were not as intense as the first and second years, but we continued with several actions that we had initiated earlier. However, some of the major changes would be made as a result of things that happened at my school.

I was awarded Teacher of the Year and my heart soared. I felt I had made my deceased parents and son proud of me, and I was beginning to feel fulfilled. Yet, I still felt the emptiness of not having Joby there when I received the award.

Graduation at my school was an emotional one for me. This would be my last graduation as a faculty member, and I would also be losing my foreign exchange student who was to graduate that year. I never thought I would be hosting a teenager so soon after my son's death, but he had been in my sophomore speech class and was having a rough second semester with his original host family.

He was from Meppel, Holland, and was one of my best students. My husband and children had greeted him with open arms. His name was Jochem Swierstra. Jochem knew of Joby because I was always open in my discussions with my students about my life and especially about living through this grief. With so many recent youth tragedies that dominate our news coverage in the media, I think it is important that students be shown ways in which to deal with this process of grief and ways in which to rebuild their own lives.

When I first brought Jochem home, I began to see many similarities between Jochem and Joby. Jochem had blue eyes and blonde hair (like Joby); he was on the golf team (like Joby); he enjoyed tennis (like Joby); and when I showed him the garden, he was shocked by the dates on Joby's grave stone. I will never forget when Jochem said, "Joby's birthday is March 18? So is mine!" We both smiled. Even though Jochem was exactly a year younger than Joby, I couldn't believe all of these coincidences—or could I?

I had made Kate's old bedroom into a guest room. I had to use Joby's old comforters and pillows for the pull-out couch. I don't think I thought about that so much then but I do now. By using some of Joby's things for Jochem, I think in a way I was bringing my son closer to me. I enjoyed seeing it all back in place. Even though Jochem was only with us about three months, he became part of the family. He was like a brother to Michael and Kate. Jochem had also befriended another exchange student at school (Quentin Thomazeau) who was from France. Quentin would also stay at our house many nights. Kate, Michael, Jochem, Quentin, and I played lots of afternoon board games and just had fun as a family. It had been a long time since my children and I had done this together since Joby's death.

I took Jochem to and from school each day. The drive in the car became our way to talk, and I enjoyed sharing with my "surrogate" son. But, the thing I remember the most is when all of us were together, we had fun without the guilt feelings. The laughter was slowly coming back into our house.

This was the first year since Joby's death that I worked at school on his birthday. Jochem's speech class adopted our tradition of launching helium balloons. They attached notes that were addressed to Joby and expressed to him how they felt about me. We all went outside and had our own little ceremony. I was grateful to these students for their sensitivity. I hope that maybe through my experience these students realized that there were positive ways to deal with grief.

We continued the scholarship during Senior Awards Night at Rensselaer Central High School; however, Joby's scholarship was given at his school by my husband Dave and my son Michael this year. I had foot surgery the week of Senior Swards Night and was unable to attend. I was glad to see them take a more active part in this action. Michael was very proud to award the scholarships. Also, the senior photo of this graduating class's top 15% was taken to join the Academic Hall of Excellence. For me, these two action steps remain important in remembering Joby, and I believe that is also true for Dave and the children.

May 18, the anniversary of Joby's death, came suddenly. Since Jochem was with us this time, I think we were just a little bit stronger through it all. However, it still was surreal; it was difficult for us to think that Joby had been gone for three years. In comparison to the first and second years, this date seem to arrive and leave more quickly. I think we were all slowly accepting the fact of Joby's death, but it was something that was understood, not talked about. Perhaps, it was because we had to deal with his loss every day of our lives, and one day didn't make it any worse.

At the end of the school year, I stood in my classroom trying to remember every photo, every poster, every corner of my room. If you have experienced a solid career

The Third Year

for any length of time, one might understand the difficulty of leaving something that once was such a major part of your life. I took down many inspirational sayings that I had hanging up in my room, pictures of my students, pictures of my family. I boxed everything for the last time. I left most of my school materials with colleagues because it was amazing how much material one can accumulate in almost 20 years. I packed the rest of my belongings in boxes, loaded them up in my Jeep, and after one last look, left the school. Many of my colleagues made my departure easier by giving me a farewell party and making the effort to individually say good–bye. I must admit, once I was ready to drive out of the parking lot, I had mixed emotions. However, the idea of not having the demands of my work was a comforting thought. I did not have to deal with the daily demands of high school teaching which would allow me more time to be at home with my family and deal with the demands of daily grief.

After school was over, I poured my energy into Joby's garden. I loved each day as I dug into the earth, planted new flowers, rearranged plants and stones, and added new items to the area. Just the daily upkeep of the garden was demanding but for me it was extremely rewarding. Each day I was able to connect a little with my son whom I could not see.

Jochem stayed with us till the end of June. The day he was to leave, Dave, Michael, Kate, and I all piled in the car (including Quentin) and drove Jochem to O'Hare airport in Chicago. When he was to board the plane, the good–byes were more difficult than we imagined. We all gave him a hug and a kiss. I was the last to say my good–byes.

I didn't want to lose another child, even if he wasn't my son. I cried and waved as Jochem boarded the plane. The ride home was a silent one. I felt I was losing Joby all over again, but I survived. As I reflect, maybe Jochem's visit wasn't by coincidence. Perhaps, his presence was a gentle reminder that I could care for someone, yet not be able to keep him near me.

Some of Joby's friends came back from school that summer and continued to help me with the garden and brought new engraved stones and flowers to plant. They also kept me informed about their own changing lives. I must admit that seeing them was a stark reminder of what my son would look like and what he might be doing at this point in his life. However, I felt the garden growing as did my relationships with these young people.

I discovered during this third year that every day would be a milestone without my son. We continued the traditions of the balloon launches and the candle lighting ceremonies at home, but I tried not to anticipate major hurdles. Joby's birthday, the anniversary of his death, and holidays without him, continued. Each day had to be dealt with. I had to find some inner strength to deal with these constant reminders. The third year forced me to look at myself and decide how I was going to live the rest of my life. I had a choice: to continue in the daily pain of my son's loss or to rebuild my life in loving memory of him. Therefore, that third year I began to take the steps to rebuild my life.

Beyond the
Third Year

Beyond the Third Year

As I prepare to put closure on this book, I am not mislead that I can ever put closure on Joby's death. Ending this book is as difficult as beginning it because I fear the existence of my child will be forgotten by others if I stop writing about him. Yet, through this devastating loss, there is so much all of us can learn. I have to ask myself: "Have I gotten over my son's death?" Of course not, but my life has gotten different, and the grief not as intense. With the death of my child, I have learned so much about limitations, extreme emotions, loss of direction, and loss of one's self. Through this journey of grief, however, I have become stronger in each of these areas: I have found new limitations, new emotions, new direction, and a new self. If anything, I learn something new each year.

After the third anniversary of Joby's death, I felt a calm within me that I hadn't felt in years. I know a lot has to do with the fact that I am not working outside the home right now. For the past three years, even the tiniest of concerns would overwhelm me, but now I am able to handle many of the daily obstacles more calmly. Even Michael, Kate, and David agree that we have been through the "worse part" of life. It is because of this insight that we own a very special "calmness" or "peace." It is difficult to explain, but with the death of a child there is a new knowledge and understanding about life that few of us hold.

The fourth Thanksgiving after Joby's death was another watershed event. That year not only was I able to attend the event, but I also managed to host my husband's family at our house! I am sure Dave's relatives are still in a daze that I was able to host Thanksgiving and survive. I had 38 people here and not once did I find myself retreating. On the contrary, I made a special toast in Joby's memory and in memory of other other relatives from Dave's family who are no longer with us. I believe I have an obligation to make sure that symbolically we do not close a door on those who have physically left this world, but remember them in tangible ways.

I can honestly say that I began once again to enjoy the Christmases with my family. It has taken a full three years of healing to reach this point, but it did finally arrive.

I have no idea if I can continue as I am, but for now it is working. I believe that I will only grow stronger. At the time of this writing, Michael is a senior in high school and that is another milestone for him as well as for us. I believe I can say that I am excited for him and his future rather than always comparing him to Joby's past. I see both of my children in a different light. Kate presently is a freshman in high school and trying to branch out as all teenagers do at this age. She has been lucky to have her big brother Michael there for her first year. Though we may now and then run into some typical child/parent battles, I think I can honestly say that I am back on track being the mom I once was. I must confess I was in so much pain those first few years, that I may have become oblivious to parts of their lives. I would have never admitted that a few years ago but, upon reflection, I know it is true.

I continue to tap into my first priority "Taking Care of You and Yours": my immediate family's needs always come first. Then, I periodically check with my Step Two

"Relating to Others" by maintaining open relationships with family and friends. Finally, I continue to renew my son's memory through my "Action" Steps by maintaining my son's scholarship, by maintaining the Academic Hall of Excellence at his school, by talking about my son, and by working in his garden.

Therefore, I won't consider this the end of my son's story but rather the beginning of a new life for all of us, including Joby. Joby grows with his garden and through our lives. The garden needs constant care and I find it to be the most therapeutic help in dealing with my grief. I am constantly weeding, mulching, transplanting, and adding new plants and nature–oriented memorabilia that reflect my son's love of life. The physical action of digging and planting in the dirt gives me a sense of rebirth and purpose. The act of gardening enables me to feel closer to life: a feeling that became almost foreign to me the day my son was killed.

The growth of this garden is a reminder of our continued love for all three of our children. As we travel on family vacations, we now bring back a little something for the garden. In this small but symbolic way, we include Joby on our trips. From my son's garden, I discovered that the journey of grief is continual and it is one of growth for all of us.

August 13, 2000 (from my journal):

The garden has flourished. I sit on the stone bench and speak softly to my son. I smile and tell him that we will be okay. The beauty of his garden is a testimonial of our struggles.

This journey is all about the little steps we take each day. It goes from day to day and things can change and turn on a dime; but one can have comfort in knowing that there are other travelers in this grief process. We are not alone in this journey.

We all grow in our individual ways. I believe once we face the loss and accept it, we begin to learn to develop because of it. For me, the stages of grief have been denial, anger, acceptance, growth, and healing. It takes time but the growth and healing can be reached; they just cannot be rushed. The changes that occur during this process may vary at different time periods for each person, but I believe that a progression of growth and healing inevitably does occur. We can help each other through our pain and help ourselves by finding something that gives us peace of mind and direction.

That is why I hope my three steps of (1) "Taking Care of You and Yours," (2) "Relating to Others," and (3) "Taking Action" can help someone in his or her own journey of growth and healing. I always try to remember that "life may not get better; but it will get different" and "different" can be good.

December 3, 2000 (From my journal):

It seems ages since I've written. So much has evolved in such a short time period of time since May 18, 1997.

Daily mourning still occurs but it is briefer, Moments of missing my son still occur, but the sharpness of its edges has become softer.

From My Son's Garden

*Can it be I am moving forward?
Am I really finding new pathways?
I cannot look back and live in the past for fear that I will not see the future for my family. This doesn't mean this journey is over; I have just taken a different road...it has been there: "that road not taken" and I am so glad I have found this path.
So, I continue to plant in the garden, in hopes that these seeds will allow my son's memory to grow and flourish.*

Healing Thoughts to Remember

Healing Thoughts to Remember

I have often been asked for advice from grieving parents or friends of parents whose children have died. That is one of the main reasons I wrote this book. It is difficult to think of everything that needs to be said. I am a firm believer that what works for some doesn't work for others. Therefore, when I make the following suggestions, they are just that—suggestions.

- Grief is physically exhausting. Get rest, even when you think you don't need it.

- Pay extra attention to a healthy lifestyle as it applies to eating, drinking, and exercising. The condition of your body can easily affect your mood swings and emotional states.

- Seek out someone you can talk to and with whom you can share your grief. Sometimes, it is better not to rely on a family member for this. (Preferably someone who has experienced the death of a child)

- You are not going crazy! Time may slip away and you may even be more forgetful than before. Hang in there; you will regain some sense of timing and purpose.

- Don't look too far ahead. Don't anticipate those holidays or birthdays. Take one day at a time.

- Don't be offended by what others may tell you. NO

parent who has lost a child will ever say, "It's time you get over this!" Remember, "it doesn't get better; it gets different."

- Try to do something physical in your child's memory. Plant a tree, start a garden, send off balloons, light a candle, donate something in your child's memory. The physical act of doing something helps keep our children's memories alive.

- Remind yourself that the intense pain you are feeling that first year or two will lessen. The feelings of grief may be daily, but won't last as long as before.

- Don't be afraid to talk about your child. Try to help others realize that when they ignore your child's existence, they only hurt you more.

- Grief is an individual thing. Remember, we don't all grieve in the same way so accept those differences. We all do what we have to do and know in our hearts what is right for us.

When I finally accepted the fact that I could not have my son back, I began to regain my life. I now do things in loving memory of him, not out of anger because he was taken from us. I have to remind the reader that the steps to healing are continual—what helped one year may have to be redone the next. From time to time, I return to this list and remind myself that I am not crazy—I am a parent who is trying to maintain some sanity after a devastating loss. I hope that my personal story of growth and healing has been able to help someone who has or is experiencing such a loss.

The proceeds of the sale of this book will go to the Joby Greene Triple A Memorial Scholarship Fund. You may contact the author at jgarden18@hotmail.com

This book was written in the memory of my son John Robert (Joby) Greene, March 18, 1981—May 18, 1997.

Joby was a happy child. He smiled with his entire face. He was a skinny little boy who was growing into a very strong young man. He was a child who wanted to please; he hated to fail; he was a perfectionist; he loved family and friends. He had a way about him that brought laughter into any situation. He was a good student; he was honest; and he was loving. Even as a teenager, he wouldn't miss out on family gatherings. He loved to be with his uncles and aunts; go on fishing trips with his dad and Uncle John and loved to play the family games of "pounce" and "dictionary" with his Hahn cousins and aunts and uncles. He loved animals, the outdoors, and sports.

In high school, he participated in tennis, basketball, golf, and wrestling. He could hardly wait until he and his younger brother would wrestle on the same team. He showed promise in a lot of what he did. He said he wanted to be a dermatologist when he grew up, so he was taking all academic courses while in high school. He had a growing interest in art and when he died, he was working on his latest drawing of Salvador Dali's <u>Persistence of a Memory</u>.

He loved his brother Michael and his sister Kate most of all. He was one of those older brothers who couldn't wait until he had a younger brother and sister. He was very protective of them and very proud of them. I see a lot of Joby in Michael and Kate.

Joby was my first born. He had my family's physical features, the blue eyes, and blonde hair. He and I had a special connection. He had exceptionally close friends, one of whom wrote me the following: "…Something I told my mom before leaving for school the day of his funeral. I said, 'It's weird. I always thought I would dress up to go to his wedding first, not his funeral. I can honestly say I love him like a brother, and I'll never forget him.' "